SpillWay

DEBORAH JENTSCH

WESTBOW
P R E S S®
A DIVISION OF THOMAS NELSON
& ZONDERVAN

WestBow Press books may be ordered through booksellers or by contacting:

WestBow Press
A Division of Thomas Nelson & Zondervan
1663 Liberty Drive
Bloomington, IN 47403
www.westbowpress.com
1 (866) 928-1240

ISBN: 978-1-5127-6049-1 (sc)
ISBN: 978-1-5127-6048-4 (hc)
ISBN: 978-1-5127-6047-7 (e)

Library of Congress Control Number: 2016917227

Print information available on the last page.

WestBow Press rev. date: 11/22/2016

FIRST WORDS

How do you define trust? We all might have some common ground in our answer to that question, based on our own experiences. A more personal question might be who or what do you trust? Again, our own reality plays into the formulating of that answer.

Within the pages of this book we share *our reality*, which at times we were unable to convince our son of. His injury caused him to believe that he was living in a dream and we needed to wake him. Time and time again we would insist—that he just trust us.

Our own trust wavered at best, in the midst of our reality. Though encouraged to trust God, we fell short in our efforts. Thankfully He knew our feeble attempts at the time were the best we could give Him, and He in turn, showed us grace and mercy.

We would be reminded that the purpose for prayer is not to receive what we want, but to receive God. Though our prayers for many days were specific, our answers whether yes or no, always involve receiving more of Him.

These words from *Spill*Way say it best:
When we went forward to take a piece of bread and dip it into the representation of the blood of Christ, I felt completely broken. It was as if

I was face-to-face with the one who understood all that I was feeling, both good and bad. It took me to a place in my heart where I recognized this was not about the Jentsch family, Caleb, or anything else we thought it was about. It was about drawing us all to that place where the body and blood had been sacrificed.

It is our prayer that you will be encouraged to trust God in your circumstances and be taken to the place of sacrifice, the cross. Join us in saying as you read, "To God be the glory!"

"Not to us, O LORD, not to us! But to your name bring honor, for the sake of your loyal love and faithfulness" Psalm 115:1 (NET).

◆━◆◆◆◆◆━◆

A special thanks to my friend Bonnie. Her encouragement and prayers moved my pen.

OUR DAYS

HE WEPT

We finished our first journal entry on January 6, 2012. Just twenty-four hours before, we were sitting in what I would describe as a large, lifeless waiting room at St. Anthony Hospital. My eyes would soon be opened to see the true details of the room, complete with its modern furniture, snow resting on the ceiling panes above, and comforting décor placed specifically to offer families a refuge as they waited. Until then, we were numb, focusing solely on Caleb's surgery, not knowing how long it would take or if he would even live through it. The possibility of death was accompanied by an overwhelming sick feeling in my stomach; the thought of getting a bite to eat was repulsive. Only those who have journeyed in the world of *waiting* in the *unknown* can relate, and none would wish it upon another during the moment.

Early in the afternoon on January 5, we skied the packed snow from our condo to the mountain's base to join the many gathered to either pick up excited children from their day's events or to catch the gondola for one last run down the mountain. The temperatures were mild to the locals but cold to Texans like us, who were glad the sunshine was beaming down to remind us cold and warmth can coexist. Kurt and I were eager to grab Sarah Kate after her completion of ski school and to get in line for the ride up the mountain. We looked prideful as we reviewed her ski school report card and praised her for the smiley faces placed by the pizza stops and turn categories.

Anticipation and excitement were building at the thought of taking on the challenge of Sarah Kate's first real ski run together. We would meet Caleb and his friends at the six-man gondola midway up the mountain and venture to the start of our destination, ending the day with a non-stressful green run back to our condo and dinner for all. Fun was on the horizon where we could all show off our skills—or lack thereof—and laugh together on the run downhill.

As I glanced down at the name appearing on my cell phone, I presumed the collegiate group was going to be a little late, and Kalina had been elected to place the call to inform me. As she slowly spoke, I wasn't alarmed when she said, "Caleb is hurt." After all, he's a good skier, and it wouldn't be the first broken bone we'd experienced on a Colorado mountain. Eric's wrist had healed without complication from his sixth-grade injury years before. It wasn't until I heard Kalina say, "Serious … life-flight him …," that the look on my face spoke volumes to Kurt, "All is definitely not well."

Instinctively grabbing a nearby resort employee carrying a two-way radio, he asked for assistance to obtain information about our son. They retreated to an area where Kurt met Keystone's Ski Patrol (KSP) director and listened as Craig delivered developing news on the mountain that would be life-changing. My heart sank—it sinks now as I recall that moment.

My first response was a phone call, and my fingers went quickly to the contacts we trusted to begin praying immediately and to recruit others to do so as well. While relaying difficult words to family over the phone, I looked into a clear, distant sky and saw a helicopter rise above a mountain peak. It was as if all the noise around me was muted as my mind tried to grasp the message my eyes were seeing. All I knew for certain was a helicopter was carrying our injured son away, and friends, family, and others were praying at that very moment. Phone calls, social media, and texts were relaying a simple message: "Caleb's been hurt skiing, and it's serious. Please pray."

Many of the next moments were a blur, yet help surrounded us. Trying to focus on coordinating our next moves to get to Caleb, Sarah Kate was being watched and protected by Keystone Resort's risk manager, who knew a six-year-old and an iPhone were a perfect match. As SK and Tracy played Angry Birds, we were told KSP's dispatch had been in constant communication with Flight for Life since their first call for help, and information was relayed through Craig that Caleb was en route to St. Anthony Hospital in Lakewood, Colorado. Keystone Ski Patrol was now escorting the rest of the skiing party down the mountain. We'd then be driven to Denver, or we could drive ourselves. Tracy assured us all other details were not a priority and would be cared for by the resort staff. Kurt and Craig's numerous calls to the emergency room finally confirmed that Caleb was just arriving aboard Flight for Life and was being hurried through a CAT scan of his head before surgery. The ER trauma doctor anxiously said to Kurt, "Get here quickly, but be safe." God was already putting His provisions in place for this very moment and for those later moments, as we would come to understand.

Five shaken college kids exited the gondola, undoubtedly scared yet reliant on their God. Paul had been their escort down the mountain and described the large cross he'd watched them paint on the gondola's fogged window, as each then took a turn to pray for Caleb during the descent. The current events weren't what they had planned months for and traveled through the night only a few days before to experience. What could possibly have prepared them for this moment in time? The strength they exhibited could only be God-given as they solemnly approached us and agreed to stay behind with Sarah Kate at our request. Handing over our skis and condo key, we entrusted them into the care of the crisis team hovering over all of us.

The roads and sky were clear as Kurt and I headed east, and our spoken words were few. My heart cried, "God, I don't want to do this. I don't want to do this!" A screaming heart and silence can also coexist, and the long silence was broken when Kurt received a call from Dr. Seale telling us that Caleb was in surgery, to be careful driving into Denver, and that we would be met at the emergency room entrance upon arrival. The trauma doc's despondent voice paused and then said, "While it appears Caleb has not sustained any life-threatening injuries below his neck, the CAT scan of his head tells a different story, and I don't know if Caleb will survive." Kurt assured him we were already praying and requested that he personally tell the surgeon the number of those praying specifically for him was multiplying—and not to worry. Though Kurt was not speaking those words directly to me, hearing them calmed my spirit.

There are some things you don't think you will ever forget. I am not sure of that, but believe I will never forget the moment we pulled into the parking lot near the emergency room and walked through those doors. I feel sure today, years later, I could drive you to the exact spot where we parked our rental car. It's similar to the dream you wish you'd never had but can't forget.

The hospital chaplain who sought us out in the emergency waiting room gave us attention others were not receiving. He guided us to another waiting area outside of trauma ICU for our peace and protection, and it was in this large area filled with empty couches and chairs that we spent many hours for the next twenty-eight days. Family of friends, and friends of friends, came within the first few hours to support us both emotionally and spiritually. You cannot fully define what a friend is until you have experienced the need for one at this magnitude.

After what seemed to be many long hours, a weary neurosurgeon and his assistant appeared, introduced themselves, and gave us their report. Dr. H. said Caleb had ultimately survived surgery and was in an extremely critical state. There were no broken bones or injured organs. The only injury was to his head—a severe brain injury—and there was still no assurance that Caleb would live. A bone flap the size of a small saucer had been strategically removed from the right side of his skull to provide the necessary room for his brain to swell. His skin was then stapled back. Starting with this evening, we would grow familiar with many medical terms throughout this journey. Cabe had suffered a severe closed head injury, and we were now part of the traumatic brain injury world.

"Wait and watch" were the instructions given to us. We attempted to eat. We were encouraged to rest. We tried to communicate. None of these attempts came easily, if at all. In desperation, we gathered up the oven-warmed blankets and pillows provided by the hospital staff and plodded in our snow boots and ski clothes to the car for the rest we knew was necessary. It was there in the cold darkness Kurt cried out to God, "Please don't let him die! Please, God, do not let our son die," and wept uncontrollably.

I have always remembered the shortest verse in the Bible—"Jesus wept"—but never had I experienced a man crying from the depths of his soul. I will never again read this verse from the gospel of John without thinking back to this particular cold night in a Colorado parking lot and to the emotion that accompanied the word *wept*. After closing our eyes and resting from exhaustion, the Colorado cold, minus the sun, was chilling our bones, so we returned to the waiting rooms to do just that ... wait.

Caleb was finally moved to a room where his personal nurses attached all the life-monitoring devices to his body and then worked determinedly to elevate the oxygen levels in his brain. Susanna and Nicole were Cabe's first trauma ICU nurses. They began treating him as if he was part of their own families, understanding his life depended on them.

2

SETTLING IN

Visitation was allowed at any time of the day or night in the state-of-the-art room where Caleb was being cared for. Our education began as his nurses instructed us on the meaning of the graphs and numbers flashing from machines by his bedside. All were connected to Caleb's body in some fashion to provide trauma nurses up-to-the-second vital information to sustain his life. Unable to concentrate on so little sleep, I focused on the screen connected to one small piece of equipment inserted through his skull—the one monitoring his brain oxygen levels.

Kurt, being the smarter of us, soaked in much more information to relay good initial updates to the many who were inquiring about Caleb's life. We realized early on, to communicate to so many people would be a full-time job, and we didn't have the energy or the time to personally employ that task. We felt a personal obligation to call our family members and the precious ones we had left behind in Keystone, and we requested they in turn send out updates through calls, texts, and social media. Much of the load of sharing initial updates was handed off to Andrea, a very well "network" connected Texas Aggie, and to brothers and sister-in-law who took a red-eye flight that arrived early the first morning. For Kurt and me, it was a welcome relief to be able to lean on someone besides each other.

We cautiously walked our family through the large trauma intensive care unit, took our right turn, and escorted them halfway down another hallway to look in on Caleb. Emotions are in a state of confusion when you're showing off what you really don't want others to have to see, yet are so very thankful to have the opportunity to still see. Not wanting Caleb's brain to work unnecessarily while unconscious, nurses encouraged us to allow only one or two people in his room at a time—without conversation he might hear—not knowing what was functioning behind his gauze-bandaged head.

Each spent some heartbreaking time with Caleb and then somehow tried their best to console and encourage us. Kurt and our sister-in-law Cindy then drove back to Keystone to get SK and our personal belongings, while our college kids remained behind to load up before coming to Denver. Four hours later, Kurt rested by Caleb's bedside, while Cindy, David, and Jim helped unpack us. Our two-room efficiency hotel was the first of two we would know as home for the month of January.

By Friday evening we were beginning to see the magnitude of movement in God's people when Jim and Pierce, two acquaintances we had never personally met, arrived from Texas to be by Caleb's side. Pierce and Caleb now had a common bond as "TBI brothers" after Pierce's head injury only six months prior, and Jim would become an invaluable resource from one dad to another after months of research for his own son's life. With help from Jim and my lifelong friend Suzanne, who was by my side the same day, a CaringBridge site was set up to share updates on Caleb and our needs for prayer.

Kurt's first entry read: "The last twenty-four hours have been emotionally excruciating for both Deborah and me. After two and a half hours of surgery on Thursday evening, the hope from the neurosurgeon was that he was more optimistic (guardedly) about Caleb's survival than when Caleb had first entered the level 1 trauma center after being airlifted from Keystone. But you have responded, and the prayers have gone up! At four o'clock this morning, a second CAT scan was performed. Not only has there been no further swelling to his brain, his brain has no longer shifted, there is no blood leakage, and only small bruises can be seen! Caleb's oxygen levels in his brain have continued to rise, with a minimum goal to reach of 20 percent. An average of 9 percent was maintained through this morning and climbed to 37 percent by late this afternoon! All other monitored and controlled functions have been managed throughout the day with minimal effort to allow his body "to be quiet" below his neck so it can concentrate all efforts toward his brain.

"Caleb is having slight 'purposeful responses' to stimuli, which is indeed painful to watch, but they are necessary to gauge his level of consciousness. All other tests for his spine and neck have come back negative. A collapsed right lung is being controlled by a respirator, which he is 'over breathing,' and that is excellent. In other words, Caleb is doing a lot of the breathing by himself! He is no longer being kept in an induced coma and is not presently sedated.

"Please continue to pray for Caleb and all physicians involved! He is still very critical, and the next four to five days are crucial to his recovery. We have shared Caleb's faith and our faith with all staff, and they know you are all praying for them as well—prayers they covet! If you didn't already know, St. Anthony is a faith-based hospital. Coincidence? We don't believe so. More updates to come from the Jentsches tomorrow!"

The prayers Kurt wrote about in the journal entry were not unnoticed. We heard and saw the evidence when our home church's sanctuary was opened for a special prayer time for Caleb. Bible verses were displayed on the big TV screens to serve as reminders of the faithfulness of our God. Caleb's promise of Nahum 1:7 was placed both on the screen at the church and on his wall at St. Anthony. This verse would make another big-screen appearance two years later back in Denver, but we couldn't know that yet. We were only beginning to get a glimpse of this promise: "The LORD is good, a refuge in times of trouble. He cares for those who trust Him" (NIV). As a circle of prayer developed on our driveway in Victoria, Texas, Pierce and Jim watched over Caleb during the night, allowing us to wrestle with a bit of much-needed sleep, knowing, as promised, they would call if necessary.

#HASHTAGFAME

Ella Bella had previously arrived at our home in her protective packaging. She was now missing, and Sarah Kate had cried for her, night after night, since the day following Caleb's injury. In the midst of Kurt and Cindy's gathering and packing up our stuff at the condo in Keystone, SK's stuffed bunny rabbit and sleeping companion had been left behind. We unzipped and rummaged through the blue luggage, the pink luggage, the carry-on bags, and all the acquired bags of our belongings, hoping we'd see what appears at first glance, only to be an old, worn-out, pink washcloth. Ella Bella was nowhere to be found, and saying good-nights are not complete unless she is in Sarah's hand stroking her face.

There had been no pink, stuffed animals in our home for twenty-two years, and none had been expected. In the fall of 2004, Caleb had burst into overwhelming tears when he'd entered the dining room to see the anticipated results from my scheduled sonogram. Only the pink balloons had still remained afloat, while the popped blue balloons laid motionless on the floor. He alone had personally filled them all with air the night before, requesting one more time to leave school and go with us for the revealing of a girl or a boy.

The fourteen-year age difference proved to be the perfect spacing for their sibling love relationship, and we knew it would be a difficult moment for his six-year-old sister to walk in and see him lying in a hospital bed wearing a gauze turban and tubes protruding from his body. She had never entered a room where Caleb hadn't recognized her with a "Wuz up?" Today would be different, very different.

Here we were, 1,100 miles from home, and away from all that was familiar. Sarah squeezed our hands tightly, being as brave as one could expect a child to be when hearing words describing a scariness she had never seen before. I was torn between wanting to protect her and wanting her to see the reality of life. The protection through prayer was evident as she walked slowly into his room and looked ever so gently at her brother. It was as if an angel had stepped into the room, and she had. Sarah was met with immediate love from the nursing staff, and she found her calling for the next twenty-eight days. Her first move as the nurses' assistant was to put a stuffed animal close to Caleb's side for comfort. No words needed to be spoken, and her ability to handle this crisis from the beginning confirmed our decision to keep her with us while Caleb fought for his life.

His tough fight began as soon as his spirit knew he was destined to live. I have no proof, but I do believe Kurt was correct when he wrote, "Caleb faced death and wanted to die, yet God announced, 'Your purpose is not complete.' We both know Caleb has a prepurchased ticket to heaven and would be fine with boarding the glory train to arrive there. He has no recollection of being spoken to by God or being called toward the light. We found our own humor in watching physicians and nurses shine a penlight directly into Caleb's eyes many times per day while calling his name loudly. My note to memory: "No wonder everyone claims to see a light and hear the call." Caleb's nonresponse was always the same, and his eyelids were released to close once again.

To borrow an expression from Sesame Street, on the second morning the number of the day was twenty. Everyone praying for Caleb was praying that the device measuring the oxygen levels in his brain would climb to 20 percent and stay above that target number in order to keep alive billions of neurons the average brain uses to function. Kurt's first CaringBridge entry revealed the number had climbed to 37 percent by Friday afternoon, and we were again moved by the power of prayer. Jessica signed the journal guestbook on January 6, 2012, 11:24 p.m.: "Wow! Prayed specifically that the O2 levels would hit 20 before the day ended. To hear they hit 37 *blew* my mind. He is capable of *more* than we could ask or imagine."

God did not have to answer a phone call from anyone to let Him know what had happened to Caleb. He didn't even need one of His believers on earth to text Him. No believer had to inform Him of the number to be reached for oxygen levels. He had known this day was going to come since the beginning of creation. He knows what our oxygen level should be down to the last digit. Yet as each prayer was lifted, He listened personally to the requests and heard the hearts of the seekers praying what Caleb had prayed for years: "Lord, show your fame to a watching world." Lydia summed up what many spoke and thought: "Caleb, you are a sleeping missionary." So as Caleb remained in a coma during the days ahead, healing was taking place in unseen places—not only in Caleb but in the hearts of many.

New generations bring new communications. I guess it is cool to be a "hashtag," although I can't say it's what I aspire to be. Caleb was said to be the hottest thing on Facebook and was "blowing up pages." My grandfather would've heard these words and wondered, "What's this cockeyed world coming to?" I try to think what that would've looked like in my generation thirty years earlier. Though it is usually used for social updates, the Facebook pages of Caleb's friends and family, and the tweets, were solely declaring the need for prayer and the answers to prayer. In the midst of the hardest days we have ever lived, God was being glorified. It was the answer to our prayer that God receive glory in our lives, but this was not the way we would ever have imagined: #prayforCaleb.

Rest, we would come to understand, is of utmost importance when recovering from a brain injury. It is not only necessary for the patient but also for those who surround him. Kurt and I realized within the first two days that it would benefit Caleb most if we made wise choices concerning our own rest. We had entrusted Caleb to Pierce and his dad, Jim, on the second night, knowing that their concern and recent experience were a provision straight from the hand of God.

As the drainage tube was removed from Caleb's skull and his vital signs stabilized, we were encouraged by what we were seeing and hearing. Guestbook excerpts from Jim and Pierce to Caleb read, "Thankful God allowed us to be here with you in your time of need, it makes our journey more complete to turn and serve you back. God has a plan for you that you are already living in your relationship with Him. This part of the journey is about sharing Him with others and glorifying Him with your walk through this ... Christ is in this and is already being glorified and shared with believers and nonbelievers, which we all know is exactly what you want as the outcome of your accident ... Just want you to know you're going to make it through this as long as you keep your head up and eyes and faith on Christ the whole time, which we know you will! You have people all around the world praying for you and your family, and most of all for your recovery ... I am here for you, just as you were for me! I love you man, and stay strong! And yes, you know I don't like hashtags, but I like hashtags calling #godisfaithful, #nothingcanstophispower, #aforsuresignwewillbeforeverlongfriends!"

THE TEAM

Accountability is necessary for most of us, and it was a no-brainer to ask the nurses to hold us (and those coming to love on Caleb) accountable to not overstimulate him. While wanting to see him respond to stimuli was the doctor's job, we were to let him rest and heal. There would be time to move and heal within the next year, but now was not the time.

Our prayers over Caleb were quiet externally, but internally they were excruciating. We continued to request ongoing prayer for Cabe's nurses and for the surgeon and anesthesiologist who would perform a tracheotomy to replace the oxygen tube running down Caleb's throat. God heard and responded yes. Kurt's entry was all caps, with shouts of "PRAISE BE TO GOD!" It concluded with "Give God the glory for the great things He hath done!" Caleb came through the procedure without any hitches, and our hearts sang along with our home church in Victoria, Texas: "May this journey be a blessing, may I rise on wings of faith. And at the end of my heart's testing with Your likeness let me wake." That was the day we continued to pray for: "Lord, please let Caleb wake."

Caleb was a junior at Texas A&M University and had been faithful to his Aggie team since he was a toddler holding up his thumb and saying, "Gig 'em." Now Caleb was a member of a new team, one not of his own choosing but of God's. His trauma ICU team on this fourth day consisted of a neurologist, nurse practitioner, critical care doctor, trauma doctor, neurosurgeons, resident physician, dieticians, his case manager, trauma nurses … and Dad. Kurt was immediately accepted and invited to each morning's consultation over Caleb, who lay motionless in his million-dollar bed.

As Caleb's prayer team seemed to increase exponentially each day, countless connections were now being asked to join in praying for him to wake up! God again revealed His plan for this day by answering the praying faithful. With vital signs holding stable, doctors now gave us permission to try to stimulate Caleb to open his eyes. So the jockeying began.

There were threats to Caleb of sending Igosians to dance in his room, uncles willing to walk on his bed singing the "I Love Tennis" song, friends pleading and feeling sure that Caleb was awaiting their arrival before he opened his eyes, and parents who longed for the Hollywood ending of his waking as they stood bedside holding his hands. Yet it was not time. Doctors and nurses continued to come into Caleb's room throughout the ensuing days and perform actions that would have caused most of us to say words outside our acceptable daily vocabulary. Doctors Mary Katherine and Phillip would call out loudly each morning, "Open your eyes, Caleb," while pinching his chest and legs or compressing the tops of his toenails and fingertips with the barrel of a ballpoint pen. Though their attempts to achieve a "general" physical response were difficult to watch and produced minimal movements, Caleb's eyes still remained closed.

Emotional pain accompanied our hope as we prayed and watched his slight response to each morning's stimuli close the fourth day by Caleb slowly "localizing" his own movements toward the vicinity of his trachea with outstretched fingers when he swallowed. Along with the discomfort of having foreign objects in his body, Caleb was running a high fever, which topped the list of specific prayer requests to find the root cause.

At the end of the day, Kurt was tired and revealed his personal weariness. He wanted to obtain an unquestionable faith in God, who says, "I am who I say I am and am capable of doing what I say I can do." Hebrews 11:1 was once again the verse he prayed for us all. Kurt's prayer continued the following morning, asking that we not miss an opportunity to see who God was working on in the midst of our circumstances, and for our obedience to personally share the Lord with them.

Kurt and "the team" met the next morning, and the results of the MRI revealed that Caleb still had brain bruises on both right front and left temporal lobes as well as on his brain stem. As the days progressed, he seemed to favor his left arm and leg with more responsive movements when requested. Our reaction to Caleb's falls throughout his life had usually been, "Get up. Shake it off. It's just a little scratch or bruise." Not this time. Bruises on the brain stem control a person's state of "awakeness" and could keep Caleb in a coma for two weeks or longer. In the meantime, Dr. H. conveyed his pleasure with Caleb's strength when localizing movements, and that a helmet fitting would soon take place to protect his post-surgery brain.

Caleb had not been wearing a physical helmet on the mountain where he'd skied five days earlier, and we still don't look back now and wish his choice had been different. We mention it here only because of what the surgeon revealed when first encountering Caleb. In Kurt's words, "Caleb was trying to die on his flight to the hospital … he was near death, and everyone struggled to keep him alive aboard Flight for Life and during surgery."

As these words escaped Kurt, God filled in the gaps, reminding him, "Death is a reality for everyone, and Caleb was ready to come home to Me!" Kurt also believed God was telling Caleb, "I am not finished with you yet, and this is way too great of an opportunity for Me to use you right now to show my glory in the midst of a difficult situation—whether it's a dad and son struggling in their relationship, a husband and wife contemplating divorce, a teen looking for a way out of this life, or anyone at a 'hard-stuff' place in life."

One guest wrote to tell us that the acronym FROG means to "fully rely on God," and each of us needs to FROG for our "hard stuff." This was confirmed as we read and proclaimed Psalm 33:22 (NIV): "May your unfailing love be with us, LORD, even as we put our hope in you."

5

FOLDED HANDS

Cleansing is considered a necessity in our culture. We take advantage of being able to choose between a shower and a bath. At every door entry, down hallways, and within the rooms of the hospital are dispensers to cleanse germs from hands. As I learned from watching the respiratory therapists, we take for granted our conscious ability to cough to clear out our lungs. Several times a day, nurses forced Caleb's body to do the same by pushing a suction tube down the hole in his throat. This was painfully hard to watch as his body would unconsciously heave up to cough and then come down gently to rest in his bed again.

Music playing in his room cleansed our minds and hearts as well. We found comfort when the nurses played "God music" on the computer, when Caleb's own playlists sat streaming on his pillow next to his head—and especially when the talented harpist played "Amazing Grace," "How Great Thou Art," and "Vision of Angels" for Caleb and Kurt. You may argue with Kurt all you want, but he not only found the harpist's music to be amazing and pure; he also believed that angels were confirming their attendance as he and nurses watched Caleb's blood pressure drop dramatically. This was just one of many ways that God revealed the opportunity to share our faith and trust in Him.

In return He blessed us with affirmations—through a doctor's name being the same as our college mascot at Texas A&M University, and through His children giving testimony of the mighty works He was doing in their own lives. We were beginning to have our spiritual eyes opened to the prayers God was answering outside the walls of what we now called "Caleb's room." Hearing and experiencing the prayers of so many, we believed we were being allowed to see what the unity of the body of Christ truly looks like and just how beautiful it is. There were many times in the midst of this dreadful circumstance when we had experienced more love and peace than life had ever afforded us before. That's why, on the day following my birthday in January, I was able to end the journal entry with the scripture from James 1:2–4 (ESV): "Count it all joy, my brothers, when you meet trials of various kinds, for you know that the testing of your faith produces steadfastness. And let steadfastness have its full effect, that you may be perfect and complete, lacking in nothing." I could honestly say, "Being allowed to see more of the landscape He is working in is amazing."

Ebb and flow, ups and downs, highs and lows were evident and part of the amazing landscape on our journey. Kurt confessed that mornings like the one on January 14 were particularly hard. His heart was broken as he got on God's case for permitting this to happen to his son. His heavenly Father personally reminded him, "I am good, Kurt, a refuge in your times of trouble. I care immensely for you because you have personally trusted in Me." Kurt's heart turned toward forgiveness and thanksgiving because he knew that God was big enough to absorb the pounding from a heartbroken father. God reassured him that He also knew exactly how he felt, and was precisely why He had used His only Son, Jesus, to provide this level of intimacy with him. The ups and downs of Caleb's physical body ran parallel to the ebb and flow of our spirits. He continues to work on building unquestionable faith. As the day ended and Caleb had rested well, we were once again reminded to "look to the LORD and His strength; seek His face always" (Psalm 105:4 NIV). We prayed to be found faithful.

"How can it be Caleb's white blood cell count has risen to 22,000 and his fever has spiked again?" my questioning heart moaned. Maybe, just maybe, a revelation would be seen in a CAT scan and spinal tap scheduled for tomorrow. As we anxiously waited for tomorrow to come, Caleb's friends and family gathered for prayer time at the Baptist Student Ministry building in College Station. As college students do, they started praying when my generation was getting ready for bed. That encouraged us, an anxious mom and dad who had spent the day watching Caleb's progress stall after struggling to fight a fever, which appeared to leave him fatigued and worn.

As Kurt retreated during the day, the Spirit provided the union of verses that he and Caleb love. "The LORD is good, giving protection in times of trouble. He knows who trusts in Him" (Nahum 1:7 NCV). The fundamental fact of existence is that this trust in God, this faith, is the firm foundation under everything that makes life worth living. It's our handle on what we can't see" (Hebrews 11:1 MSG). And so we were able to move from one day to the next, knowing God is true to His word and speaks to us "in the darkness and whispers in our ear." We were thankful for each new day, and tomorrow morning would be one where we found it easier to give thanks.

Kurt's arrival at the hospital was greeted by the work of the Holy Spirit—who, by the way, requires no sleep. Caleb's temperature was down, and his heart rate and breathing were good. The doctors were ordering an MRI to accompany the other scheduled tests for the day. All was proceeding nicely this morning, but the revelation we awaited came in the form of dreams by three different people during the darkness. The nurse on morning duty had dreamed about Caleb the night before and his eyes were open. Anxiously entering his room, she saw that Caleb's eyes were still closed but was gifted with an even more compelling visual of his hands clasped together as if he were praying.

As we thanked God for this, we remembered His Word imparted to us through my oldest brother, John. Isaiah 45:3 (NIV) says, "I will give you hidden treasures, riches stored in secret places, so that you may know that I am the LORD, the God of Israel who summons you by name." We clung to this verse, knowing even if we couldn't communicate with Caleb the way we desired, nothing could keep God from communicating with or through him. We felt led to pray that Caleb would remember clearly all God had taught him in his twenty-one years of life, and that he would receive riches in secret places with his Lord.

On January 17 Kurt summarized it best in this entry:

> "Whoever has my commands and keeps them is the one who loves me. Anyone who loves me will be loved by my Father, and I too will love them and show myself to them" (John 14:21).

Thank you for again loving the Father by praying for Caleb, for He has loved you back by showing Himself to you today!

I got to Caleb's room early again this morning for our quiet time of devotion and prayer with the Father. A quick scan around his room's abundance of monitors eased my anticipation … and why should I be surprised, for over three hundred students gathered to pray specifically for Caleb and to worship the Father on the campus of A&M last night, with additional hundreds of others praying from their homes at 9:00 p.m.! Blood pressure, breathing reps, heart rate, and yes, even temperature had all been well under control for most of the night … Cabe had experienced a great night under nurse Jill's compassionate care!

As Cabe and I finished up our time, nurse Kate came bursting through the door, smiling from ear to ear with an honest radiance on her face that I wish each of you could have seen. When she'd arrived for this morning's shift change, nurse Jill had come to her and said, "Come, Kate. You have to see Caleb!"

Entering Caleb's room, she'd found his hands not only clasped together (as Deborah reported earlier today) but also with fingers interlocked as if he was praying. I smiled and said, "No doubt, Kate," and then proceeded to share with her and the physicians what had taken place the evening prior as hundreds collectively lifted Caleb up to God and asked Him to move. And move He did, because at Caleb's current level of consciousness, this was an absolute, no-question-about-it "purposeful movement" Caleb himself has not repeated to this degree today! It was truly one of those deepening-of-the-faith, blow-me-away moments I believe was more for all of us than for Caleb. God was saying, "I love you … continue to pray … I have Caleb's situation well under control!"

Caleb had a pretty full day of testing, including an MRI and spinal tap. The CAT scan performed yesterday did show some increase in fluid on the brain when reviewed this morning, and it looks like the culprit for the infection may be coming from his brain. The number of physicians attending Caleb grew by one this afternoon, with Dr. M. (infectious diseases) being added to the mix as another pair of eyes and consult. Caleb's spinal fluid showed a high increase in white cells, where you or I typically have only three to five cells total. White cells fight infection, and the high number means there's an intruder they're after. Cabe's sugars are also down in his spinal fluid, which indicates a potential form of bacteria has developed. Cultures are being grown over the next three days.

The good news is that God is pointing us to the source of the infection (pray specifically that there's only one), and Dr. M. has already begun targeting with one of two high-powered antibiotics, which will begin at midnight tonight. PTL! The second will begin in the morning with the goal of Caleb improving by Thursday or Friday. Dr. M. is an extremely sharp lady, and Deb and I have full confidence in her abilities after visiting with her. (Please add her to your pray list.) She will begin "rounding" with Caleb's physicians tomorrow morning. Caleb is also having fewer secretions from his lungs, with no more coughing (on his own), and it looks like the pneumonia has been blasted away by the other antibiotics. Please continue to pray for his kidneys and creatinine levels, as it will take some time to assess any damage from the strong antibiotics. He is young, and kidneys at his age are very resilient. He's passing a lot of fluid, but that does not mean his kidneys are filtering as they should.

If you've ever watched any TV episode of House, you pretty much get a picture of how I've felt over the past eight days in trying to pinpoint the source and fight against Cabe's infection. (Sorry for the bad comparison, docs and nurses, if you're reading.) The key difference (and not a bad comparison) is that Christ is nowhere to be found in this made-for-TV series. Again, I cannot begin to describe the depth of relationships we are making among the staff, and the faith discussions we are seeing "come out" as more and more get to know Caleb—and as we meet with other families that have similar physical needs. Please pray for Deb and me, that we will not miss any opportunity to serve Him while we're here with Caleb. I believe God is always at work around us, and the obstacles that once kept folks from desiring a relationship with the Lord can shrink and get very personal in times such as these.

Thanks for loving our Lord (Nahum 1:7; Hebrews 11:1).

6

THE ROMAN ROAD BIFECTA

"for all have sinned and fall short of the glory of God … For the wages of sin is death, but the free gift of God is eternal life in Christ Jesus our Lord" (Rom 3:23; 6:23 ESV).

As elated as all of us were to see and hear about Caleb's "purposeful movement" of clasped fingers this morning, God's plans are always much larger than the way we see our circumstances, and they are always designed for His greater purpose. Nurse Rachel's questions to Kurt about God and the Bible were fast and inquisitive as she attended to a routine check of Caleb's vitals. As Kurt's eyes began to open to what the Father was doing, he silently prayed to rely on the Holy Spirit and not mess up any of His answers.

Their conversation quickly moved to God's unwavering love for humanity, and His plan to turn a fallen, sinful world back to Him. That rebellion against God began back in the garden of Eden, and it was never intended to be part of the relationship He still wants to have with each of us today. "For God so loved the world," He would make a Way for His most cherished creation to be in right standing with Him once again. He allowed His only Son, Jesus, to die for all humanity's past, present, and future rebellion.

As Kurt moved through God's plan of assurance, I entered Caleb's room to hear a familiar gospel presentation about God's love and redemption through scripture found in the book of Romans. Catching Kurt's eye, I smiled as I pulled his requested morning's Diet Dr. Pepper from my bag, along with another purchase after multiple stops on my way to the hospital. The purchase was a gift from a Christian bookstore, but I'd had no idea at the time why I was buying it. Little did Kurt know that my smile reflected a "God opportunity" already developing before my arrival.

Upon Kurt's completion, I revealed a cup adorned with colored stripes encircling it. They told the story of God's personal plan for each of us, from beginning to end, using some of the same Bible verses that Kurt had just shared. Both versions had been presented to Rachel, and she thankfully received the gift of the cup.

Making our own decision about beginning a relationship with the Father after hearing or reading His Word is our choice. Our free will to choose is still God's plan, and although Rachel did not make the choice to accept God's gift of His Son personally, we know seeds were sown and spiritual eyes were opened this morning. We were thankful for the opportunity to see God at work in the midst of our lives and to be part of His plan. Tomorrow would be another of God's "planned" days when we would see the open eyes we had long waited for.

CLASS OF 2013

The most exciting update that we'd announced since the first few, came on the thirteenth day of Caleb's journey. It had to be reported in all caps, because the proclamation was to be shouted from Denver, Colorado, to Texas and beyond.

Written in CaringBridge on January 18, it said: "PRAISE GOD!!!!!! CALEB HAS OPENED HIS EYES SEVERAL TIMES THIS MORNING AND IS RESPONDING TO SOME COMMANDS! STAYED TUNED FOR MORE UPDATES (Nahum 1:7: Hebrews 11:1)."

This is the update that followed later that evening, written by Deborah Jentsch

January 18, 2012, at 6:27 p.m., titled "In the Potter's Hand."

> The enemy is frustrated. I had almost completed the update and was seeking a verse to complete it before I posted it. The site froze, and for at least thirty minutes on low battery, I was trying desperately to figure out how to thaw it out—only to

have to leave the page and lose my post. Oh, Satan, as I told you this morning, the battle belongs to the Lord, and you are defeated! So get thee hence Satan, for it is written that you shall worship the Lord your God, and Him only shall you serve (Matthew 4:10 KJV). Jesus has won the victory, and you know your days are numbered.

I have enjoyed thinking on the heavenly perspective of this journey, especially today as angels watched Kurt make his way to the hospital to have a time of quiet with the Lord and Caleb. As he read to Caleb from the devotional *Jesus Calling*, by Sarah Young, about ascents and descents and the sun shining on snowy mountain peaks, Kurt was reassured of God's call on this journey.

After completing his quiet time in the room, Kurt called me at our hotel room to tell me that Caleb had opened his eyes slightly. When asked to open his eyes, he had opened them completely. Kurt asked him to grasp his hand and squeeze it if he could hear him, and he did! This was a time of celebration, tears, and praising God (which many of you have expressed to us through messages throughout the day). For those of you who have been praying and seeking God in this journey, *please* know that God hears your prayers, no matter what answers come.

Caleb has continued to make purposeful movements throughout the day, and they've had to restrain his hands to keep him from pulling at his trachea. His vitals have been good, with fever remaining down. His white blood cell count is down from 22,000 to 12,000. His kidney functions are improving, and the staples were removed from his head today. Tomorrow they will drain fluid from the brain area. The targeted antibiotics for a brain infection seem to be working.

Caleb's "Jesus Music" playlist was cycling through his songs on his phone. "Never Let Go" came on, and it just seemed so *utterly* natural to the small choir of six in the room to gather round and sing "Oh no, you never let go ... through the calm and through the storm ... every high and every low ... You never let go of me." Caleb was snapping his fingers slowly and slightly throughout the day—and definitely during the song. He responded to command movements at times by sticking out his tongue and doing a fist pump. We are hoping to see more of this in future days.

For the Aggies, class of 2013, following in this journey, this is the thirteenth day, and Kelley had texted that Caleb would open his eyes on the thirteenth day. KK said, "I called it." We are just thankful he is from the graduating class of '13 and not '80 or '81 (although they are among the best for Kurt and me).

A friend of mine commented this morning on our great faith, which is best summed up in the words of another: "I have a small faith and a great God." Kurt and I have a small faith and a *great* God. In Matthew 17:20 God's words say it best: "If you have faith as small as a mustard seed, you can say to this mountain, 'Move from here to there,' and it will move. Nothing will be impossible for you."

"For this light momentary affliction is preparing for us an eternal weight of glory beyond all comparison, as we look not to the things that are seen but to the things that are unseen. For the things that are seen are transient, but the things that are unseen are eternal" (2 Corinthians 4:17–18 ESV).

While we celebrated Caleb's "eye opening experience," there were those around us who would not be celebrating for their own loved one but would instead be preparing to say good-bye. It only took a glance over the nurses' command post and across the hallway to see the painful experience of friends and family gathered for one who had also met injury on the majestic Colorado ski slopes. As Lu and I visited with a dear friend of the injured, we prayed for the "eyes of the heart to be opened." We experienced the answer today as Don entered the room carrying his Bible and asking to pray over Caleb. We continued to see God at work all around us, and we thanked Him for the opportunities.

SHARK BITE

While intently watching someone breathe in and out may not be on the to-do list for most people, we found great pleasure in it. As Caleb breathed without a ventilator for over five hours, he also snapped his fingers strongly and loudly to the beat of the music playing over his phone's speaker. It was close by his head where he could easily hear it, and it reminded me of his days in the preschool church choir and being told, "The boy has rhythm." Therapists and doctors chuckled at his constant snapping, never having experienced it before.

With Caleb's eyes closed and fingers moving, the occupational therapists commenced working over every major muscle group in Caleb's body and wore our boy out. His worn-out body also responded well to the harpist's return to play beautiful songs of faith again, which we needed as much as Caleb. Watching him now pull slowly and forcefully against his wrist restraints for two solid hours elevated his heart rate and ours, causing us to wrestle with God over what we were seeing right before our eyes.

Our grappling was only heightened as the doctor's hefty syringe removed 160cc (5.5 ounces) of spinal fluid from the enlarged soft part of Cabe's head, and to even look at him from his right side was painful. Per Dad's word picture, Caleb's head looked much like a shark bite, withdrawn and severely indented as the fluid was slowly extracted through the large needle. He thought Caleb would also think it looked cool, since shark week was always a time of male bonding around the television in our household.

What Kurt couldn't know at the time was how much we'd talk about sharks in the upcoming months as having been a major part of Caleb's dreams. We were not running marathons, climbing mountains, or wrestling grizzly bears, but we were tired and felt as if we had been. Our souls needed rest, which came through prayers, posts, concerns, and acts of kindness from so many people who loved us—or more importantly, loved God.

9

BEING REMINDED

After a tiring day and a good night's rest, joy came in the morning. Caleb opened his eyes on command for the neurosurgeon, slowly raised two fingers for the neurologist, and squeezed and released the hand of the infectious disease physician. What an incredible showoff—and we welcomed his performance!

The neurologist said he was but one step away from being back with us. The CaringBridge entry summed up the larger performance: "I just stand back in awe as this is happening, not only for Caleb but for the way the physicians, nurses, and techs are responding, and for the *pure joy* they seem to be experiencing in his responses. God is truly at work through Caleb to bring Himself the glory. I cannot wait to see what He is going to orchestrate next!" Oh, the thrill of those moments when we celebrated the victories we were praying for. In days ahead it would be critical to keep our eyes on God, our orchestrator, because at this time, we couldn't even begin to know what was coming down the road. There would be much in our days ahead that we did not like—finding those days extremely difficult to get through.

We enjoyed the high notes we were experiencing for this day, and we gave thanks for them. On this sixteenth day after his injury, Caleb had an awesome day, making it very easy for Kurt to be happy with God and what He was doing. During the day's brief rest, he was reminded, "Relax, be still, and know that I am God in all of Caleb's days. Our relationship is no different today from what it was yesterday or what it will be tomorrow." This was not a new revelation to Kurt or me. God had shown this to us in circumstances before. He was willing once again to reaffirm this truth because of His patience and love for us.

As each of Caleb's days showed steps of progress, we spent the moments soaking up the time we now treasured. Kurt spent time rubbing Caleb's feet, legs, and stretching his arms, and in response, Caleb's blood pressure would drop noticeably. The antibiotics for the infections appeared to be working, holding his temperatures slightly above normal. Doctors were already scheduling surgery to replace Caleb's bone flap, which was being kept cool in the hospital freezer for the time being. These are not the normal things you think about every day. Yet what we were now having to think about every day had been dramatically changed through our "life interrupted," which caused us to center on more than our circumstances or ourselves.

We chose to follow a Sunday routine we've practiced for most of our married days and attended a worship service in a nearby community. The service did just that ... it served us well. It served us with a message from God that said, "The purpose for prayer is not to receive what we want but to receive God." Though our requests for many days prior had been very specific, our answers always involved receiving more of God. Emotionally spent and being in a place of worship was somewhat of a slight struggle for me, knowing that we had come to receive comfort.

When we went forward to take a piece of bread and dip it into the representation of the blood of Christ, I felt completely broken. It was as if I was face-to-face with the one who understood all that I was feeling, both good and bad. It took me to a place in my heart where I recognized this was not about the Jentsch family, Caleb, or anything else we thought it was about. It was about drawing us all to that place where the body and blood had been sacrificed. I wept uncontrollably and hurt very deeply.

As the services ended and we reflected on the many prayers being taken to the cross of Christ on our behalf, we gave thanks for those who were praying for the first time in a long time. It allowed us to turn our mourning to joy and sing with the congregation "Be My Everything." We sang from the depths of our being, pleading for God to be our everything.

10

A MODEL PATIENT

Caleb was scoring high on the Glasgow Coma Scale (GCS), which is the most common scoring system used to describe a person's level of consciousness following a brain injury, and for the succeeding days after emerging from a coma. He was scoring high on charts that recorded his body's functions. He was now sitting in a recliner, opening his eyes, and responding to verbal commands with slow, purposeful movements. He was scheduled to have his bone flap reinserted four weeks ahead of medical expectations by the same surgeon who had removed it. And plans were already in the works to transport him from Denver to our home state of Texas.

As parents who had prayed for this time, we should have been ecstatic. Yet the relationships we had built and the care we had received had become our new comfort zone, and it felt good to be comfortable. We had become so secure in the comforting arms of God during this time, relishing the opportunity to grow personally in our God-trust. Our decision now was to either stay in the Denver area or return to Houston, Texas, for the next stage of rehab. Even though Houston was not our home, it was closer to our home, friends, and family, and it offered a sense of security that we knew wouldn't be readily available in Denver.

So we once again prayed for faith and courage for the days ahead in the unseen and the unknown. This was another opportunity to say, "I trust you, Jesus," as I had encouraged Kurt to do on January 4 when he'd mixed up his rental skis with another pair at the Keystone lodge area. I was reminded of being able to trust Jesus with a lost pair of skis, but I was struggling to trust Him with my precious son. That was not adding up in my spirit.

The God who had planned and knitted Caleb together in my womb also knew the number of hairs on his head, and He was by far the most logical choice of whom to trust. After all, I know nothing about replacing brain flaps, flying a helicopter, nursing, rehab, and all that would become necessary in Cabe's recovery— let alone knowing the number of hairs on his head. We put our trust in the One who knows all this and more. So requests were put out for prayer that Caleb's replacement surgery would go well and to give thanks he would not require a helmet for physical protection after all.

Just as Kurt held tightly to Caleb's hand, God held tightly to Kurt's hand. Caleb had his eyes fixed on his father as he read the *Jesus Calling* devotion and then tightened his grip during Kurt's prayer for him. Kurt prayed for Caleb to have strength to put aside any fear or anxiety that was present, and to trust the One who does not give us a spirit of fear. At *amen*, Caleb was looking directly into his father's eyes, his hand still holding tightly to him when the anesthesiologist arrived. We waited and rested in John 16:33 (NIV), which says, "I have told you these things, so that in me you may have peace. In this world you will have trouble. But take heart! I have overcome the world."

We all love to hear our children praised, and we especially loved hearing the post-surgery report from Dr. John describing Caleb as a model patient. He felt the procedure to reinsert a piece of Caleb's skull with tiny plates and screws could not have gone any better, and Kurt smiled. His smile was not just to say we were happy, but to affirm that prayers offered for the surgeons only hours earlier had been answered in a way that said, "You can trust Me." As Kurt relayed the message through our community of followers, he thanked them for sharing in the unknowns and for continuing to exercise their own faith to believe.

Following Caleb's surgery, we still found ourselves mostly just watching and praying. With hours to sit and watch comes the opportunity to listen. In listening we heard the words Jesus spoke to His disciples. "Keep watch and pray, so that you will not give in to temptation. For the spirit is willing, but the body is weak!" (Matthew 26:41 NLT). We were witnesses to a weak body, and we watched the heart-rate monitor confirm Caleb's heart was working much harder than the norm after his surgery.

Your heart rate is often a good indicator of what's going on inside your body, both physically and mentally. Our lifelong family habit of rubbing feet was beneficial in lowering Caleb's heart rate a bit and helping him to rest more easily after a few hours, so we took a short break with Sarah Kate to give her some quality time back in our room.

Kurt's arrival later in the evening was met seeing Caleb's heart-rate back up to higher levels. It was a beautiful sight to behold when the monitor's numbers quickly declined twenty points at the sound of his dad's voice just ask, "What's up, Cabe?" This is what we define as a blessing. It's an experience that allows us to see through physical eyes what happens in a spiritual relationship with our Father. He tells us to watch and pray, to listen to His voice in spite of our circumstances. When we do stop to listen and hear, our heart rate will always drop, requiring much less of our own effort to find more rest in Him.

While resting in the Lord, Kurt also found time to rest in The Bed. We like to call it Caleb's million-dollar bed, which is precisely why we don't own anything even close to it. On most days Caleb was transferred from the bed to the recliner via a "pea pod" harness and overhead hoist to spend at least four hours in recliner therapy. To keep his bed warm, Kurt took the opportunity to assume Caleb's usual position, dozing off with the finger massage and swaying mode in action. It was quite entertaining for the trauma nurses peering through the windows, and Kurt was thankful for legalities that prevented them from snapping any pictures. He jokingly thanked them for warding off the respiratory therapists who may have mistakenly wanted to suction his lungs as well. While both Kurt and Caleb enjoyed their new positions of rest, Caleb's vital signs were actually doing better while also reclining.

With the daily improvements increasing, we put travel dates on the calendar and made arrangements to leave. The Bible verse that spoke to this day was from the book of Exodus, which is where we get our word *exit* from. And He said, "My presence will go with you, and I will give you rest" (Exodus 33:14 ESV). This verse was true for the Israelites; it was true for us on January 5; it was true for this day; and it would be true for the many unknown days ahead of us.

FROM UNCOMFORTABLE TO COMFORT TO ...

It continues to be so evident to us the words of God we've heard and learned throughout our lives are words of truth. They have become very personal to us in our time of need, and in light of the Truth, it made sense to me that being in need of God is a blessing. As the time neared to leave Denver and the daily routine and comfort we had experienced, the unknowns were now staring us in the face. We knew where we were headed, but we had very little clue as to what it would be like when we got there. In our minds it was mostly just a geographical change, but we would learn this was not true.

I have found for myself that operating in the unknowns works out better on my behalf. In other words, the less I know, the less I know how to mess up. I find myself instructing God on what to do when I know too much. God chose to speak specifically to me today with a psalm that simply says, "Be still and know that I am God..." (Psalm 46:10 ESV). With details still to be worked out, He gently reminded me of His orchestration of details over the past three weeks and encouraged me to enjoy each one. In this time of stillness, Caleb had been without pain medicine since the day before, and he was on his last bag of antibiotics.

Our treat came when his smiling nurse arrived with a wheelchair and oven-warmed blankets for his first trip outside—not just outside his room, but outside the hospital where he could breathe the fresh, cold Colorado air deeply. The hope was the atrium experience would spur Caleb to realize a near ending to the longest hospital stay of his life, as he seemed to soak up the crispness and flora of his field trip. Our stroll circled the long way back indoors to his room and included a stop to see the chapel.

Ornate with beautifully milled timbers against stonework and stained glass windows, a circular stone ring, six feet in diameter was suspended from the middle of the chapel's ceiling. Carved deep into the stone were the *large* words "Be still and know that I am God." *Unbelievable*, I first thought. There are over fifty-four thousand verses in the Bible, and God had decided to show this one to me twice in one day? We don't consider these coincidences; we prefer to call them winks. God wants to reveal much to us intimately in many ways, and we believe the Bible is undoubtedly one of those ways.

We thought Caleb might be experiencing some anxiety after returning to his room, because he appeared to retreat within himself by ignoring us. You can never know what another person is thinking unless he tells you, and since Caleb hadn't uttered a syllable for twenty-two days, we could only guess. My heart ached for what he might be feeling at this moment as the reality of where he was and what had happened to him was possibly starting to occur.

We were reminded to adopt a big-picture perspective and not let today's details bring us down. So we turned once again to capture the view outside our townhouse stairwell during the afternoon and remembered Psalm 121:1–2 (NAS) telling us to "lift our eyes to the mountains; From where shall our help come from? Our help *comes* from the LORD, who made heaven and earth."

The descent from our hotel room to the parking lot provided a view of what lay off in the distance. There I stood in an enclosed cold stairwell, viewing a distant mountain. I pulled out my cell phone to take a picture to remind me you can view life beautifully from wherever you are. I could choose to look down at the worn carpet, or I could look at the window-framed view ahead. The mountainous snow-covered terrain reflected the sunlight, and a calm fell over me. I knew once again God was revealing His truth—this time through His creation. This was but one day, with many ahead that held many more opportunities to choose what, or whom, to focus on.

BRAIN PICS

Caleb would have his brain picked in many ways. Another MRI was ordered, and the picture showed a little bleeding around his bone flap, which we were told was not significant and would resolve itself with time. As the nurse practitioner came into his room to share the imagery, she noted that Caleb still seemed more responsive with his left hand than his right, and favored looking to his right more than his left. Before that could be logged into her notes, Sarah Kate came casually walking into the room after her social time with her nursing buddies.

Caleb's eyes were intently focused on her every move from the *left* side of his bed, transmitting pictures to his brain of every bite she took from her toaster pastry (Pop-Tart). She too had learned the routine of testing Caleb, and she asked him for a "Gig 'em" (a thumbs-up, for non-Aggie fans). He responded appropriately with both his left and right thumbs. Sarah even jumped into the action when the speech therapist worked his vocal cords over by offering her brother ice chips to soothe his throat. The therapist was very encouraging and excited at Cabe's early stage of recovery, as he readily responded to her commands to try to sound vowels.

Along with his alertness were bits of frustration and irritation inherent to every brain injury, which would intensify during his recovery. We empathized with Caleb having to listen to his mom and dad talking to him so much. He even seemed to close his eyes during these moments as if to say, "Please stop!" He did seem to enjoy the time we spent together the next morning, however, as we shared a daily devotional. It was my time alone with Caleb before Sarah and I boarded our plane to Houston.

We had more bags packed for departure than when we'd arrived because of all the gifts that had been bestowed upon us. The most special gifts, however, were the ones we were leaving behind, and it was hard to say good-bye to friends and caregivers we had become so close to in such a short period of time. Caleb was sleeping soundly when the time came for us to make our move toward the airport, and Sarah Kate woke him to tell him good-bye one last time. As I leaned close to ever so gently tell him we were leaving, his mouth opened wide … and he yawned. All those observing laughed, and as I too laughed, I cried.

Approaching the airport, it was as if God had cleared the pathway for our departure. Kurt was able to get us checked in at curbside, and we breezed through security and boarded the plane to have our choice of a window and center seat. Sarah Kate quickly befriended the lady sitting next to her and soon began telling her all about Caleb. It came as no surprise to learn that she was a pastor's wife from Texas and a wonderful

God-gift. She took my hands into hers and prayed for Caleb's healing and our peace.

Our plane rose above the land where we had spent the past twenty-four days and took us to a land closer to our home. For now, we would call Houston home.

13

A PREPARED PLACE

There is a verse found in the Bible in the book of John, chapter 14, where Jesus tells those He is with that He is going to prepare a place for them and will come again and take them there. I hadn't taken these words literally at this time in my life, but that was exactly what God had done.

Though my parents lived near enough to the rehab hospital in Houston to commute daily, we were offered a much closer location to make the back and forth easier. Instead of a thirty-five-minute drive plus additional time needed for Houston traffic, we were invited into a home within ten minutes of the hospital with very little worry about traffic. Lee Wedgeworth had e-mailed me during our stay in Denver and introduced herself as the mother of one of Caleb's friends. She explained to me the convenience of where they lived in relation to TIRR Memorial Hermann Hospital, and the availability of not only a room but also a car, since her daughter was on a mission trip out of the country. Thinking this sounded nice, but leaning more toward the comforts of Mother's care and Daddy's breakfast, we planned a site visit to be sure of our decision.

God confirmed that He was at work in the planning as soon as I met Lee and immediately fell in love with her. I love people who are real, and she and her family are the "for real deal." Lee and John had only occupied their lovely home for the past year when they agreed to offer us their spare room, the sharing of their kitchen and den, the fourth-floor getaway, and a car of our choosing. Who does that?

We felt sure that the Spirit of God had moved them to open their home to us, as well as moving Sarah Kate, who was hesitant at first but was all-in once given directions on how to use the elevator. These are not people who live in luxury and can afford an elevator for pampering's sake. They too had been through life's trials in earlier years and had found their trust in the Lord to be not only sufficient but also abundant. John had been in an accident while shredding some property and had spent many years in rehab. They not only offered their home but also their experiences and what they had learned through them. These were the kinds of things we could've never put a value on but were provided to us along the way. The credit card commercial says it best: "Priceless."

Though we were not settled into their home just yet, we did settle on being their new tenants for however long it took.

HOUSTON, WE HAVE A PROBLEM

While Sarah Kate and I were working on the Texas transition, Caleb and Kurt were making a move of their own. Caleb was being stepped down in nursing care, moving from his room to the third floor, from trauma care to ICU. It had been decided that his current level of nursing care in TICU was not now needed.

Only the day before, God had reminded Kurt that every single circumstance of our lives was under His control and He was working all things out to bring Himself glory. A few moments after returning from taking Sarah and me to the airport, emotion flooded him as he pulled into the same parking space he had on January 5. Today it looked much different, and going home appeared to be the next step. His grateful thoughts were interrupted by the noise of Flight for Life's turning blades gaining speed on St. Anthony's rooftop to head toward another circumstance where God would be fully present—and, hopefully, allowed.

Caleb's alertness and anxiety were increasing each day, and today he seemed agitated, trying to say "catheter" along with the nurses' requests to vocalize the words *hi* and *bye*. Kurt was definitely the better caregiver at this time, because he could empathize with his son in a way a mother could not. Kurt also handled the scheduled travel day delay to Houston better in person. It was being postponed for two days because Cabe's hemoglobin count was too low. Two units of whole blood were typed and cross-matched to help Caleb reach the minimum blood oxygen levels required by TIRR before admitting him.

In hindsight I came to fully understand why TIRR wanted him to be ready to hit the ground running (well, not exactly running) with his tennis shoes on. With the additional blood came color and an increased energy level, boosting Caleb's movements against his restraints much more so than in days previous. Trying very hard to verbalize words before Kurt placed a call to my cell phone, we were both gifted with hearing Caleb work to say softly, "Hi, Mom, I love you," for the first time. Anytime someone tells you they love you, it's like receiving a welcomed infusion.

A text from my friend Iris said, "God is knocking our socks off." And He was. I was reminded in my daily Bible reading of God's rescuing the Israelites from the hands of Pharaoh. In the book of Exodus, the message to His people was, "God will certainly come to help you…Don't be afraid. Just stand still and watch the LORD rescue you…and the LORD Himself will fight for you."

My sincere response was to agree with what I read and to remember that my Father in heaven also wants to hear "I love you." Some days are harder than others, just as they were for Caleb, but we must utter the words the best we can.

TEXAS BOUND!

Kurt and Caleb traveled thirty-five thousand feet above the earth from Denver to Houston on a private medevac jet. Their time in the air was considerably less than that of Sarah Kate's and my commercial flight. This was a good thing, because the trip was stressful for Kurt and the nursing crew after Caleb's agitation lasted all but the final twenty minutes. We had grown accustomed to this behavior pattern from traveling with children through the years. Our kids usually fell asleep about twenty miles from our destination, which always proved to be the best twenty minutes of the trip. You could tell from Kurt's face that he'd been put through the wringer as the single caregiving parent for the past several days. It definitely confirmed our need for each other.

A transport ambulance met their flight at Houston's Hobby Airport upon touchdown and brought them directly to TIRR where we anxiously awaited their arrival. Oh, the joy it was to see Caleb with eyes wide open as the wheels of his stretcher opened toward the ground in Houston, Texas. Born-and-raised Texans tend to be prideful and think the rest of the country cannot live without them, but our pride was tempered with thanksgiving for those we had left in Colorado and for being in our home state. It just felt good and right to be saying "home" again.

The comparison of our two flights home seemed to parallel Caleb's state of readiness between Denver and Houston. We were now moving on a faster "plane" at TIRR than at St. Anthony, and all passengers on board needed to be trained and ready for therapy. Kurt had already accomplished the transition from "nurses watching around the clock" in trauma ICU to an "available hands-on nurse" checking in on a fixed schedule. It was a new transition for me. As Kurt took a much-needed retreat to Baytown, Texas to sleep and be loved on by family, I was experiencing the prescribed transition. While Caleb and I awaited therapy, Kurt was experiencing a therapy all his own as our ninety-plus-pound Goldador, Jazzy, loved him as only a dog can. The licking and lap hugs were just what the doctor ordered.

My uncomfortable chair-bed in Caleb's room was perfect for the first night, allowing me to be by his bedside in new surroundings with a roommate we grew to love. It didn't take long to realize that Caleb didn't like resting in his new, unsecured bed. He would randomly rise up and then have to be coaxed to lie back down again. It was much like trying to coax a toddler to lie down for a nap, but TIRR was prepared for times such as these. Caleb's hospital issued bed was exchanged for an enclosed net bed, which I think to be one of the greater inventions in life. I'm sure there's a reason baby beds aren't already made like this, but my thought was how perfect it would've been during those sleep-deprived nights of the baby years.

Where Caleb's hands had been restrained in Denver to keep him from pulling and tugging on tubes and wires, they were now free to do whatever in following the no-restraint policy at TIRR. This meant keeping a watchful eye on all activities behind the zipped net, and being ready to unzip the side panels in a hurry if Caleb didn't follow the verbal instruction, "Don't pull on that!" Mitts placed on Caleb's hands were provided to assist in pull prevention, but we proudly witnessed Caleb work to manipulate his to freedom. In spite of the consequences, we rejoiced at his ability to do so. To us it just meant his brain was beginning to figure things out. Caleb received freedom not only from his hand restraints but from his catheter as well. This too would require more work on our part, yet once again God provided a capable group of caregivers to assist Caleb and to teach us how to help in the activities of his daily living.

The daily routines picked up their pace. I had been doubtful when first told that Caleb needed to have his tennis shoes and gym clothes on the very first day. After all, the last pair of shoes on his feet had been ski boots—twenty-eight days before. But they weren't kidding. The physical therapist arrived early the first morning and was motivated to start. To put it simply, Caleb wasn't going to be encouraged to lie on his backside all day.

Speech therapy twice, occupational therapy, and the neurological psychologist's evaluation followed physical therapy each day. At this point I was convinced Caleb must have been tired, because I knew I was, and I proved it. During an initial round of questions, the psychologist asked me Caleb's birth date to use along with two fictional dates to test the severity of his memory loss, which we were learning was almost a given following any TBI. Each morning Caleb was asked to identify his correct birthday—along with what color tie the psychologist had been wearing the day before, and the current year, month, and date. I simply responded with 10/18/2000.

Before Jerome could quiz Caleb, he would, of course, need our son's actual birth date. A puzzled look crossed his face as he surmised that Caleb was obviously older than twelve. After being made aware of my confusion, I correctly answered 1990, and within the same breath told him he might have more to work on than just Caleb! At the end of this long, tiring day, the urge to look backward came, and I remembered the tears and the pain.

This was the psalm given to me at the completion of this very hard day: "You turned my wailing into dancing; you removed my sackcloth and clothed me with joy, that my heart may sing to you and not be silent. LORD my God, I will praise you forever" (Psalm 30:11–12 NIV).

16

TESTING

Evaluations are necessary tools used in all areas of life, and the team of therapists, doctors, nurses, and caregivers all played a vital role in evaluating Caleb before they began treating him. His results determined the specific course of his therapy and care, and part of his evaluation included a swallow test. Caleb liked their decision that thickened nectar and pudding would now be added to his diet. It was the first food he would eat orally in over a month. His own words, which were not understandable most of the time, were crystal clear in a deep monotone voice: "Pudding would be good." Kurt and I both laughed as we joyfully fed him a few spoonsful for the very first time.

Even as we were seeing advances in Cabe's recovery, a strong fear began to develop in us. In the past month we had been required to watch and pray, and we had focused solely on Cabe opening his eyes. Now our own eyes were being opened to what might be required in the days ahead, and we wondered if we were up to the challenge. We had willfully moved our focus from our Provider to our circumstances, and we were in need of refocus. Refocusing became our own "therapy" for many days and months to come, and it would require our deliberate efforts.

Only months earlier, I shared an example of what God had shown me with a young woman as she was preparing for college. I asked her to mark her left hand as her *circumstances* and her right hand as *God*. I instructed her to place her left hand in front of her right hand and to tell me what she saw. She answered, "My circumstances." Reversing the order, I then asked her to place her right hand in front of her left hand. She knew the question, "What do you see?" and the answer, "God." When we focus on God, we cannot focus on our circumstances and vice versa.

So Kurt and I moved God back to His rightful position and prayed about the days ahead. He answered us in Isaiah 41:10 (NIV): "So do not fear, for I am with you; do not be dismayed, for I am your God. I will strengthen you and help you; I will uphold you with my righteous right hand." This Bible verse, spoken so many thousands of years before, was exactly what we needed for this day.

SINGING OFF KEY

With so many people following Caleb's journey through the CaringBridge site, our whereabouts was no secret. Requests to visit Cabe were numerous, and it was especially difficult for me to say no, knowing the sincerity of the hearts of those requesting. We were advised not to overstimulate Caleb, and with a naturally overstimulating family already, we only allowed a few to visit at a time.

Our new location on day four didn't go down in the books as one of our favorite destinations. We had offered grace when Caleb pulled the feeding tube out of his stomach the day before as his "one on one" was trying to stop him from going after his trachea tube at the same time. We hadn't become angry, knowing it could've happened to anyone caring for Caleb. Upon our arrival on this particular morning, however, a doctor was evaluating a rising knot on Caleb's forehead in the same general vicinity as his injury. A CAT scan was ordered to make certain no damage had occurred after striking a nurse's leg brace as she caught him rolling out of his bed.

Now we were angry and frustrated. To add to our frustration, radiology was experiencing technical difficulties, and a transfer to a nearby hospital to complete the imagery presented us with admission difficulties. We would learn more about our personal filters as this journey progressed, and we gave thanks that it was one of those times when we knew better than to verbalize our actual thoughts of "What else can go wrong?"

Many hours later we were back in the room, and therapies for the day were a no go. We willfully chose to be merciful to those who were working hard to serve Caleb—and allowed our anger to be directed at God. As we had seen and would see in many days ahead, God was big enough to handle our anger and then turn right around and show us His love with mercy and grace.

Nothing said it better to us than a smile, and just a short while later, we all witnessed Caleb's first one since the morning before his injury. His cousins were making their initial debut when his beautiful cousin—who had "smilingly" posed in photos with Caleb through the years—excitedly entered his room. He looked at her, and in a very serious and still monotone voice, said, "You are ugly!" We all laughed after he had followed my directive so well, quickly adding with his own smile: "Just kidding." This gift came from a loving God after a very trying day.

And if his smile wasn't enough, we sat in amazement as Caleb recited John 3:16 later in the evening. He then broke out into a flat toned song, and a small ensemble—Kurt, the nurse, and myself—joined in. The nurse pulled up songs on her phone, and the boy who had only said "Hi, Mom" days before was singing these words: "I'm trading my sorrow, I'm trading my pain, and I'm trading it all for the joy of the Lord."

Our joy, stolen from us that morning, had been returned to us by evening. The troublesome CAT scan proved to be another blessing, showing that not only had no damage occurred after tumbling from his bed that morning, additional healing had already taken place since the last scan at St. Anthony. A scripture became personal when we inserted our own experiences of the day. "Though the mountains be shaken [though your son bumped his head] and the hills be removed [and he removed his feeding tube] yet my unfailing love for you will not be shaken nor my covenant of peace be removed, says the LORD, who has compassion on you" (Isaiah 54:10 NIV).

We kissed Caleb good night, and my tears and words said, "I am so sorry." I felt like I had let him down, not protecting him from the pulls and the bumps. I deemed myself guilty for not keeping a constant eye on him. Yet with only the explanation God had laid on our hearts, we continued to leave Caleb in the evenings under the twenty-four-seven watch-care of the hospital staff, believing that God wanted us to trust Him with the rest.

This was easier said than done, and the releasing and trusting would be tested over and over again as we traveled on this journey. At the end of this particular day, we thought we knew and believed enough about God to be sure He was not looking the other way when Caleb bumped his head—as much as I'd like to think He possibly was. He just doesn't do that.

Standing and waiting for the elevator after telling Caleb good night, Kurt asked me if I was okay, and my most honest answer was "No! I am mad! It's not going my way!" And in my heartache, I cried once again. So, in a warring of emotions, I left the hospital with Kurt, and we devised a plan allowing Kurt to be at the hospital before Caleb woke and became agitated by his surroundings or the attachments to his body. I confessed my heartache to our followers the next morning in an early update, posting: "His eye is on the sparrow, and it most certainly was on Caleb."

Our plan worked great. Kurt wheeled Caleb into group therapy in the gym and then on to Sunday morning church service in the rehab's sanctuary. Kurt reported all had gone well, and that Cabe had prayed in his best vocal effort and had sung with the group. I was in absolute awe to learn the song he'd sung was "His Eye Is on the Sparrow." People may call such things happentance, but we know better. God had just given me these very words, and then my son was singing them. This song would find us again in a future place—a place we had no idea existed, much less knew we would be going to.

On this day it was time for me to stop and thank God. I first had to thank Him for testing me in what I believed. How tragic would it be to find out what you say you believe you really don't—and when the time comes to put your faith into action you freeze in fear—or worse, turn and run away from the Promised Land? Testing is necessary to reveal what you really believe and know. We had been—and would continue to be—tested in the words God commanded to Joshua: "…be strong and courageous! Do not be afraid or discouraged. For the LORD your God is with you wherever you go" (Joshua 1:9 NLT).

CALEB IS MAD

Caleb wasn't mad at the results of the Super Bowl game between the Giants and Patriots. He slept through the whole game, and we were reminded that he wouldn't have remembered the final score even if he had watched every play. When I entered Caleb's room the next day, he was sitting in his wheelchair with an unmistakably sad face. His eyes were closed, he was silent, and his head hung down. He would not have been considered for a "camper of the day" award.

The personal evaluations he was being put through by medical staff were not settling well, and he feared that his scores were not high enough. His speech therapist boldly asked if he was mad, and Caleb stated angrily, "I'm mad at the situation." Abby calmly proceeded, working in a spirit that included so much more than her mere occupation. She asked Caleb to read the verse printed on her "Pray for Caleb" bracelet. He quoted Nahum 1:7 and then read it aloud three times from the printed poster on the wall: "The LORD is good, a refuge in times of trouble. He cares for those who trust in him." His speech continued to improve noticeably, as did his countenance, with each repetition.

As the day advanced, Caleb's spirit was being renewed and transformed by God's Word. Not only was it a full day of therapies, but Cabe experienced some physical changes as well. We were all very surprised when nurses removed the fifty-third staple from his head. We hadn't realized so many had been used to suture his skin back over his bone flap. He also received a non-cuffed trachea tube, which gave him a new and stronger voice while still being used to breathe through.

Caleb was so proud of his new-sounding voice, he began deejaying his own radio show from his net-bed, asking listeners to tune in to 95.1 and 89.3. Kurt happily recorded the performance as a future reminder of just how far a road we'd traveled, while we were both being entertained by a personality we hadn't seen since Caleb's accident—one we would savor into the tough days ahead. This day is in my memory as one of our favorites.

The days seemed to become extremely long, with Caleb's emotional fluctuations and physical requirements demanding much of us all. Our stamina was being tested by his recovery, and we didn't want to neglect Sarah Kate and her needs. Sarah was enjoying the "it takes a village" program put in place, because those in her village were loving her well. The way we were feeling was once again best expressed in the devotional *Jesus Calling*: "The journey has been too much for you, and you are bone-weary. Do not be ashamed of your exhaustion. Instead see it as an opportunity for Me to take charge of your life. Remember that I can fit everything into a pattern for good, including the things you wish were different. Start with where you are at this point in time and space, accepting that this is where I intend for you to be." The passage continued to speak exactly to what we needed to hear as exhaustion settled in.

Seeing Caleb's demeanor vary from hour to hour was quite different from the mostly quiet-filled days in St. Anthony Hospital. We both prayed over and over again that Cabe's hope and desire for God still took charge of his life and would not be lost as his brain worked to reconnect through rehab at TIRR. We began to see Caleb emerge from the inside out, and those caring for him were our witnesses. He continued to randomly break out singing Christian songs, reciting scripture from memory, and praying aloud for those he felt led to pray for—all with his best efforts. We had no doubt that God was ordering Caleb's footsteps as he responded with "I love You, Jesus" or "Thank You, Jesus" at just the appropriate times.

And Caleb's reward couldn't have been greater. As the music therapist strummed her guitar, the four physical therapists accompanied his first steps. Supporting Caleb's torso from the front and behind, and his legs from rolling stools on either side, they literally lifted and moved his legs and feet to a continuous beat, walking slowly in their combined strength across the room. As an audience of two parents watching their encouragement, we couldn't have been prouder again of our son's first steps. Yet we saw more than just Caleb this time. We saw the bigger picture of the overwhelming support we were receiving from believers who persisted in holding us up in prayer as we moved our own steps forward with the Holy Spirit's guidance.

The icing on the cake was hearing Caleb say, "I like this place," after being placed back in his wheelchair. Within the hour, back in his room, Caleb spoke again: "I don't like this place!" Like Caleb, we forget so quickly. We understood his forgetfulness, and we believed our Father in heaven understood ours as well.

19

THE ENEMY IS AWARE

It looked like the revelation of Caleb's victory was becoming more and more apparent with each passing day. And every day we counted his challenging improvements and changes as the *best*. It appeared our enemy also recognized what was going on. I hate to think about the celebratory party he threw on January 5 when a faithful servant of God laid motionless, speechless, and fighting for his life. So, when Satan, the father of lies, started seeing life and hearing truth, he seemed to call in his forces.

The title given to a daily entry in our messages to friends and family was titled, "It's a Lie." Caleb was undergoing a lot of therapy in Houston, and after twenty-eight days in Denver, his brain and body were now becoming tired and stressed at TIRR. We all know how being tired and stressed can be so very taxing on us, even without a brain injury, which usually affects our thoughts and actions negatively. Caleb was beginning to say things that were not true and to have destructive thoughts. His attitude spiraled downward, and we found ourselves fighting to keep our heads above water. We began thinking about the what-ifs of our future, and we became discouraged.

Not only were our thoughts being attacked, but our personal possessions as well. It was crazy! Kurt's work phone began to have letter issues when texting or e-mailing. It was as if during the night four keys had switched places on his keypad, and though the words he typed were incorrect, he had typed them correctly. For example, when he typed the keys for w-a-t-c-h, the screen showed "zqtch." Fortunately, there was a rescue plan for resolving the issue from the help desk. Their response was, "Unfortunately, I've never heard of this issue. Overnight the phone to me so I can have it in my hands."

What a reminder this was for Kurt and me! The phone's jumbled letters illustrated what Caleb was presently experiencing in his life. There was much confusion in his thoughts, though all the data remained intact. His condition was best described by his neuropsychologist: "Caleb's file cabinet has been spilled out on the ground, and a lot of files just need to be put back into their proper place." Things were mixed up and coming out of Caleb as erroneously as they were on Kurt's phone, yet he too would find healing while remaining in the hands of the Master Healer. Amidst the confusion in his brain, Caleb was still able to compose a text (on his own phone), place a phone call to a friend, and ask his therapist if she knew Jesus. For those still-organized "files," we gave thanks.

In order for neurons to rewire and refire within the brain, Caleb was frequently engaged in questions and learning activities. This meant we had homework to work through with Caleb in the evenings and during scheduled downtime. Not only were we being trained to help cognitively, but Kurt also graduated in transfer techniques used to move Caleb between his wheelchair and bed to the shower and bathroom. I was much more apprehensive about that, and I stuck to the homework duties, asking for help in assisting Caleb if Kurt wasn't handy.

With increased duties, we welcomed Cindy's offer to spend the day with Caleb and let us focus on SK for a few hours. Aunt Cindy was a trooper, participating with Caleb in therapies and then returning to his room to watch old movies and read to him as she had often done when he was young. He was blessed by her company. He also enjoyed cousin Ryan when he showed up to strum and sing some T-Swift songs. Both Cindy and Ryan were truly the hands and feet of Jesus to us. We were reminded of what Mark said in chapter 10, verse 45 (KJV): "For even the Son of Man came not to be ministered to, but to minister."

Groups of friends started coming for weekend visits, and Caleb had moments of much laughter. It was fun to hear him reminisce about times spent with each, even though he confused the details of their relationships. On one particular weekend it was obvious Caleb identified with almost everyone as someone he'd known in Paris while traveling with iGo Global Ministries during the summer before his accident. When correctly reminding him they were his recent classmates at Texas A&M, Cabe smiled broadly and said with added expression, "No way! Really?" Due to the absence of his short-term memory, this tangled conversation occurred over and over again throughout their afternoon visit— as it would throughout our many days ahead.

We summed up the weekend by recalling Caleb's antics. He had smiled, smirked, scowled, played, sang, and rested. He displayed signs of brain overload after becoming confused and frustrated when trying to keep everything straight, only then to lose what he had remembered just minutes before. He expressed nervousness and asked many questions. There were many questions for all of us, but few answers.

The hard days were unrelenting and became progressively harder as we watched our son's agitation increase from moderate to extreme. God's provision at this time was in the form of a room available next door with no roommate. Caleb's roommate was not a problem, but Caleb's aggression was becoming a hardship for both his caregivers and for us. Whether his brain was rejecting the reality of being brain-injured or not, "a dream" was the best description of how he felt. Caleb was in a world of post-traumatic amnesia—aka short-term memory loss—and every moment of new memory was quickly lost or confabulated with the current events in his surroundings.

Fortunately, Caleb's long-term memory hadn't been altered and remained mostly intact. However, it conflicted with the reality, as he literally believed he was in a dream, and no matter what wonderful picture we tirelessly tried to paint of his reality, he wasn't having any part of it. Our best efforts to assure Caleb fell on deaf ears, and he became angry when we wouldn't awaken him at his request. His actions became manipulative, and he didn't act accountable at many times for his harsh words and acts; after all, it was just a dream. We had to work hard not to take his actions and words personally, knowing that his heart had never before allowed him to speak or act in such a manner.

It was on one particularly tough day when Caleb's caregiver confirmed our feelings that a spiritual battle was taking place.

Caleb swung to strike a caregiver from his bed position. We kept the bed panels zipped and locked during these extreme times to prevent Caleb from hurting himself and others. Our consolation after his actions came with the almost immediate heartfelt apology following each outburst, revealing that he still knew right from wrong. He then held no memory of either response, which had occurred only moments before.

Our hearts literally ached on the day we physically held Caleb down to the bed while he yelled out in anger, "Go get my real mom and dad! You are only the parents in my dream!" Later we would laugh at the novelty of our new title, "Dream Parents," but at the time, laughter was in a far and distant land that we were not experiencing. Once again we found peace in what we currently knew as the hardest times. Peace and hard times can coexist, and we believe it's because Peace is a person, not a feeling.

One of our greatest moments of knowing peace was yet to come during a sleep study Caleb would undergo to determine if any seizure activity was present.

20

FEAR AND PEACE

Many days were over-shadowed by fear while we were at TIRR, both for Caleb and for us. We recognized that Caleb's fear was increasing as his awareness surrounding *his own reality* became more relevant, openly sharing it with us and others at the moments when he was most fearful. When pain was inflicted on his body during a therapy session, he feared that someone was trying to hurt him, so he pulled that someone's hair very hard to let her know she was hurting him. Upon realizing what he'd done, his immediate response was once again "I'm sorry" and "I don't know why I did that."

Learning about brain injuries can be harder on the learner when the occasion is real, as opposed to just reading words written in the pages of a book. We were learning that there is a grueling cognitive progression in brain-injured patients after comparing Caleb's current behaviors with those categorized by the Rancho Los Amigos Scale. Kurt prayed to see from Caleb's perspective and to understand that his fear and nervousness were a "good thing" to see. They were the unfortunate steps of the healing process toward full recovery. As God had done so many times before, He provided exactly what was needed for this day. The Word of God from *Jesus Calling* said, "On the evening of that first day of the week, when the disciples were together, with the doors locked for fear of the Jewish leaders, Jesus came and stood among them and said, 'Peace be with you!' (John 20:19 NIV)." Kurt vividly recalled our thirty-ninth day before, understanding what the disciples had felt when gripped by fear. Peace arrived for the disciples, and we prayed that Caleb would know the peace he held with Him.

My personal fears showed up in ways different from Caleb's. You might guess that I, being over fifty years old, have learned to mask my fears very well. When Caleb was asked if he knew what special day it was on February 14, his quick response was, "Thanksgiving?" We kind of chuckled at Cabe's answer and then were reminded that it really was a day to give thanks. Then we came back to the big question it left in my mind: "Is this as good as it's ever going to get?" I found myself asking that question many times over.

God continued to answer patiently, and an answer came through a parent of another TIRR patient from a few years prior. My daddy attended a basketball reunion at Texas A&M and visited with a coach whose son's recovery after a brain injury had progressed well. Through their conversation, he assured us Caleb's responses were similar to those of his son. Recognizing the uniqueness of traumatic brain injuries, we knew this was not a guarantee, but a calm assurance. We liked to believe it was best that Caleb lacked all of his short-term memory at this point anyway, because remembering from one moment to the next might allow his fear to become more pervasive. So we rejoiced when Caleb's college roommates came to visit and later requisitioned additional wheelchairs to play basketball outside. We were thankful Caleb had no fear of what they thought or how they might perceive his condition. He just lived in the moment, enjoying it until tiredness set in, and then he didn't hesitate to tell them he was done and hugged them good-bye.

21

SUNDAY THERAPIES

Sundays provided a much-needed therapy of their own. TIRR's church services were so uplifting and suited specifically to the needs of the residents. Caleb and friends attended services downstairs in a large, open room filled with other patients and their families. Most, like Caleb, were seated in the same wheelchairs that had transported them to the sanctuary. All were belted in and confined to their chairs, which made singing the next song even more beautiful. While most sang with passion, "My chains are gone, I've been set free," the lyrics took on the purpose they were meant for. I'm not sure how much the time of worship meant to everyone else in the room, but for me it was the comfort and reassurance I needed.

Sitting outside the facility after lunch, Caleb was sad because his observation concluded that all the people at TIRR were sick. At first judgment, one would agree with his assessment. However, the truth was most people left TIRR in much better condition than when they'd arrived, and the snapshot of a point in time was not a valuable tool to make a healthy judgment, especially when you were a resident.

Caleb's next days were filled with the depression that comes with recovery, and when asked how he felt, he replied, "I feel stuck." He likened it to Jonah being stuck in the belly of the whale. We also recalled Joseph being stuck in a palace prison. Neither of those places was desirable. Thankfully, these biblical accounts didn't end there, so we could experience the hope of becoming unstuck. I related it to times in my life when, like Caleb, I wanted to close my eyes and quit, because the events in my life were not fun, and I too felt stuck in an unhappy place. Kurt and I recognized that the words *fun* and *good* were not necessarily interchangeable. Many times in our lives, what was good for us was not fun. The scripture we relied on was from the book of Psalms. "Give thanks to the LORD, for he is good. *His love endures forever*" (Psalm 136:1 NIV).

We knew God was good, and we knew He would be with us for the long haul.

22

FEARFUL, NERVOUS, AND RESTLESS

Believing God was in control, and adding the things that we were seeing in Caleb, did not equal the good results we were desperately hoping for. If God was in control, why was Caleb becoming progressively more fearful? His actions now were those of a paranoid individual, and the best we could determine was that he feared never waking up from *this dream* he believed he was in. He went so far as to ask to use my cell phone. I didn't know who he was calling or why he wanted to use my phone, but I was impressed by his thought process.

Caleb pushed the numbers on my phone to call his own, and with a solemn utterance, he left himself a message: "Remember to find out how to get rid of these dreams. Okay, bye." I wish written words could somehow convey the expression attached to them. When Caleb spoke the reminder, it was like something you might see in a movie where the detective strategically leaves a voice memo to himself.

After Caleb hung up, Kurt started doing his own detective work. He handed Caleb a cookie, told him to taste it, and then asked him to determine if he believed it was real or not. Caleb agreed it was the real deal as he swallowed each bite, but he wasn't so convinced that it wasn't just a real cookie in his dream. The best words we could tell Caleb were, "You will have to *trust us!*" No sooner had we spoken these words, the same were spoken directly back to us from our Father in heaven. "You perceive fear, and you witness nervousness, and the results are restlessness. But you are going to have to *trust Me.*" We also remembered the Bible verse we'd heard many, many times in our Christian lives: "Trust in the LORD with all your heart and lean not on your own understanding;" Proverbs 3:5 (NIV). Had our trust been plotted on a graph throughout this journey, observers would have seen both high and low points dotted above and below God's trend line.

At one of my low points of trust, though I probably didn't identify it as such at the time, I devised a medication plan for Caleb. The plan was based on what I had observed in Caleb throughout the past few days and on the meds that had already been prescribed at TIRR over the last five weeks. The team of doctors reluctantly acquiesced to my requested new plan of action, but it only took one act of extreme agitation from Caleb for me to want to scrap my plan altogether. We stayed the course, trying to help him pass through another period of agitation and aggression, but one particular Saturday was not progressing well at all.

With friends in town from College Station to attend the TIRR Memorial Hermann Rodeo, we really wanted to help Caleb enjoy the time spent with them. The biggest obstacle to helping him do so was his adamant refusal to leave the security of his bed.

Nature called, and Caleb was helped to the bathroom. Seizing the opportunity to redirect his thoughts toward getting into his wheelchair instead of back into his bed, we overcame his comfort zone to steal the moment we needed. He was wheeled to the rodeo in the gym to play games, which—he quickly made it known—he did not want to participate in. He was a passive, unwilling participant for about an hour before he let it be known that he'd had enough. He became aggressive toward me, reaching out to strike. He then proceeded to angrily tell me that he did not want to be here and that he did not want to do what they were asking him to do!

Everything inside me wanted to scream, "I DON'T WANT TO BE HERE EITHER!!," but refraining, I took him to his room instead and helped him back into his zipper bed. He asked everyone to be quiet so he could sleep, and soon spoke a farewell to his friends. Really, it was a ploy so they would leave, and after their departure, he took my hand in his and cried. In deep despair he asked three questions: "Why is this happening? Why am I dreaming this? Will you pray for me?"

I could only answer one of the questions, so we prayed. As I said amen and opened my eyes, Caleb kept praying. The exact words he prayed are not etched in my memory or written down for me to remember, but I do know that he asked God to heal him. He asked God to help him know what was real and what was not. He pleaded to be heard by God—that God would know he was *really* asking, not just saying some words. He finished his prayer by asking God to be glorified, and he hoped his life wouldn't continue to be so hard.

At this point, the prayer time wasn't yet finished. Kurt pushed the door open quietly so as not to disturb Caleb if he was resting, and was greeted by Caleb asking him to pray also. These were moments we are able to look back on and store as treasures. As Kurt expressed often, "Most dads don't ever get to spend moments like these with their twenty-one-year-old sons."

After such a long and trying day, we encouraged Caleb to rest. Instead he phoned a few friends, and his demeanor appeared to change. Kurt extended an invitation to support Caleb in walking the hallways, to which Caleb quickly agreed. This was a polar shift from his morning's desire to stay in bed, and we were encouraged to see his willingness to participate in a therapy walk this evening.

My mind began to churn back over my plan, trying to figure out what I thought was right about it and what was wrong. Fortunately, the Holy Spirit paused me mid-thought and whispered, "Caleb's prayer was heard and answered, and it had nothing to do with your plan." When the Holy Spirit humbles you, it is a gift.

As I read *Jesus Calling* the next morning (February 26), I was in total awe of the words: "I am leading you step by step, through your life. Hold my hand in trusting dependence letting me guide you through this day. Your future looks uncertain and flimsy— even precarious. When you try to figure out the future you are grasping at things that are mine. This, like all forms of worry, is an act of rebellion: doubting my promises to care for you."

I sat amazed that a single devotion could speak so directly to our circumstances. Watching Caleb move step-by-step while depending on his dad to hold him up was directly related to what

I had just read. After having devised a medication plan for Caleb on my own, the words "You are grasping at things that are Mine and this is rebellion" convicted me of how I was exerting my plan over God's. The truth was, I didn't like the way His plan was looking. The devotion concluded by saying, "Relax and enjoy the journey."

JUST GRINDING IT OUT ...

Since we were not boarding a cruise ship, and circumstances didn't appear to be improving as fast as we wanted, relaxing and enjoying weren't a state that we usually found ourselves in. In spite of our dilemma, however, we were seeing small evidences of improvement in Caleb.

Caleb was clinically trying to press forward, and Jerome helped us understand what might be occurring in Caleb's brain. He likened it to a NASCAR race in which fifty drivers fly around a mile-and-a-half oval track at nearly two hundred miles per hour, ready to push through a calamity of events at any given moment. The drivers understand that while they'll suffer occasional nicks and bumps that come with a five-hundred-mile race, their goal is to mentally find a way to push forward through each of those difficult moments as they present themselves—and finish the race.

At this time, Caleb's brain was becoming awfully nicked up by the speed at which things were moving, and lost in a number of crashes holding his attention—rather than pressing forward through most of them. The fuel these cars run on is also extremely important, and most run on a mixture designed specifically to make them operate at peak performance. Caleb's team of doctors was working hard to find the correct combination of meds to help his brain ease forward with the least amount of trouble. The scene reminded Kurt of a passage of scripture in Philippians. Even with all the adversity he was facing, the apostle Paul still said, "… By no means do I count myself an expert in all of this, but I've got my eye on the goal, where God is beckoning us onward—to Jesus. I'm off and running, and I'm not turning back" (Philippians 3:13 MSG).

I guess it's the same with the trial-and-error process of maintaining race cars. It also became evident to me that the current medications were not helping to produce the desired results in Caleb's behavior. He left scratches on his one-to-one caregiver during the night as she granted one of his seemingly sincere wishes. His second request of her received a different reply. She told him, "I may have been born at night, but not last night."

During a morning's psych evaluation over breakfast, Caleb expressed to Jerome his need for something to drink while eating in his unzipped bed. Trusting Caleb—and then immediately realizing he should've known better—Jerome handed Caleb a carton of milk, only to find himself quickly doused after Caleb took a sip. Caleb was exhibiting extreme agitation, and those in close proximity of him were the victims.

Following his early morning outbursts, Caleb went about the rest of the day producing good work, both cognitively and physically, and was ready for dinner upon returning to his room at 4:30. We were able to wheel him downstairs to the dining hall for a change of scenery, and then back up to his room when he was ready to be showered. He asked questions he had asked before about his crash on the ski trip. He asked why he couldn't remember things, when he would depart from TIRR, and when he would return to A&M. Kurt and I found it ironically comical that he wanted to know locations and exact dates in answer to these questions (and untold others), because within moments of answering, he couldn't tell us the correct day of the week, what month it was, or the year we were living in. We understood the revolving pattern that Caleb didn't. We also realized that he would probably ask us these same questions again tomorrow, and the day after, and the day after that ...

When tomorrow came, we arrived and hid in the background. One theory was that Caleb was possibly becoming too dependent on our presence and might do better if we backed away. We watched from a distance as his therapists and caregivers worked to coax him out of his room and on to therapies. This required their combined efforts, and nurse Jerri stood on constant standby, ready to administer a shot at the first sign of any extreme agitation. We were comfortable with this strategy, not only for the safety of those working with Caleb, but also for Caleb himself.

As Jerri came toward us with tears in her eyes, I felt sadness for her. She was crying, and I immediately assumed that she hated having to give Caleb a shot. I was wrong. Instead she shared the overwhelming peace that had overcome her as she listened to Caleb sing songs of praise during his therapies.

All at once I saw the beauty of this scenery: Caleb was in therapy and singing praises; Jerri was experiencing a peace only God provides; Kurt and I were being reminded by God that this journey had a greater purpose than what we could see; and two caregivers were acknowledging something they had never witnessed before. In the middle of the hardest days of our lives, God was allowing us to see a bigger picture of how He can use all things for good and for His glory.

24

CAT SCAN, UNPLANNED

Caleb was not scheduled for a CAT scan. Like many other unpredictable events along the way, it happened anyway. Following a good night's rest, a breakfast of champions, and a neuro-psych evaluation without throwing his milk, this day was off to a pretty good start.

Upon our arrival for lunch, Caleb was being wheeled back after completing not only physical therapy but also speech therapy with Abby, who, by the way, still reintroduced herself to Caleb daily. His new fashion for the morning included garments of outerwear for protection. He had a protective mask covering his face and protective mittens on both hands. These were not for defensive gear. He was also sporting a red mark on his forehead, much like the faded birthmark he'd had as an infant. This was unnecessary confirmation for us that Caleb must honestly believe he was stuck in a dream and not real life.

For the second time, Caleb had taken on his nurse, who is solid and fit and well over six feet tall. The first time he went after Nick was in response to Nick calling him Jason in his heavy Jamaican accent. Caleb had verbally attacked Nick, struggling to reach him with arms swinging wildly as he sat strapped to his wheelchair. Today Caleb took a different approach for a different reason, but his target was the same.

Nick and Mo had awakened Caleb from a brief nap to complete his therapies, and while they were transferring Caleb to his wheelchair, he seized the opportunity to express his disapproval and head-butted Nick. According to the doctors, Nick had taken the worst of the blow, but another scan was ordered to make sure Caleb hadn't caused a secondary injury to himself.

In the waiting, where we were so often finding ourselves, the clinical manager for the sixth floor sat with Caleb and listened intently as he asked her our same questions. In her calming voice, Deanna repeatedly assured Caleb that he was not living in a dream, and that his experience was real. Though Caleb wasn't convinced she was correct, he showed no aggression and only finally asked if he could pray with her before she left his room. Gathering herself to leave, Deanna slowly stood with tears streaming down her face and said, "Caleb, you are so special. God has a bigger plan for you, and part of it was meant for me today."

We had been told that we would have to be the lighthouse to lead Caleb through the post-traumatic amnesia he was living in. After Caleb touched Deanna, we began to wonder who the lighthouse really was. After all, the scripture from Isaiah 42:6–7 (MSG) says, "I am God. I have called you to live right and well. I have taken responsibility for you, kept you safe. I have set you among my people to bind them to me, and provided you as a *lighthouse* to the nations, To make a start at bringing people into the open, into light."

No doubt, the evidence was pointing to Caleb.

THE ENEMY LURKS

Most people long for their children to be in the top 10 percent of their class, so when it's reported they're in the top 5 percent, parents should be ecstatic. As doctors collaborated early this morning, they agreed Caleb's scores lay within 5 percent of all TBI cases that are tough to discern and treat because of his moments of both lucidness and incoherency.

There were moments, however, when the look in his eyes caught our attention and was very disheartening to us as parents. We had just recently read that Satan sees things as an interest, a concern, or a threat. Although we believed at one point in time Satan was not willing to risk entering into our journey full force, many involved saw it differently now.

Not knowing if his swing in behavior was a reaction to medicines, brain shearing, fatigue, or whatever, we were on a trial-and-error regime. Caleb would be removed from all medicines—a clean slate, if you will—to capture a picture of where he was without them. He was able to sleep and rest well, but he still woke up tired and agitated. As with other plans, it was short-lived, and before the next morning was over, he was being given a shot to take the edge off. It took a while for the calming effects to occur, but it made for a much better day.

Caleb began to ask a variety of different questions—besides the repetitive ones dealing with dreams versus reality. He began to make inquiries concerning what was wrong with him and when he would be better. He still wanted to know his exit date from TIRR, but on one particular night he seemed content to stay there—after eating a full order of Pappasitto's sopapillias brought by his aunt and uncle. Caleb made the request to get up and walk off a full stomach. He said, "I want to walk like I did when I came in here." We helped him out of bed for an assisted walk with Dad but didn't have the heart to tell him that he'd been nowhere near walking when he'd arrived here on a stretcher.

The next day Caleb was still motivated to walk. While Kurt stepped out of the room, leaving Caleb zipped in bed, I preoccupied our son by talking to him on the phone from the Wedgeworths' home, which allowed Kurt to confer with the neurologist in the hallway. Caleb must have noticed a gap at the top of the zipper and decided not to share that important detail with me before we hung up.

No one was aware of Caleb's movement until Kurt turned around and saw him in the doorway heading toward him. He wasn't in his wheelchair, and his unsteady steps were following the sound of his father's voice. His desire was to be with his dad and not be left alone in his room. It was where he wanted to be, and he was willing to take great risks to get to him. We breathed in thankfulness that Caleb didn't fall and hurt himself.

We exhaled gratitude for his ability to achieve what he hadn't done in recent weeks.

We looked at this somewhat scary event and saw a lesson to be learned. Recognizing our Father's voice allows us the freedom to move toward Him, taking the steps we are supposedly unable to take. Risks and fears will almost always accompany them, but we must be willing to unzip what is holding us back and rely on Him to move us in the right direction, even if our steps are unsteady.

As I pulled into the medical center area later during the day, music on the radio provided a timely message to me through two songs, which proclaimed, "Greater things are yet to come and greater things are still to be done," and "Strength will come when we wait upon the Lord." Caleb had just finished one therapy, and another had been cut short because of his agitation. Following the doctors' recommendation, we put Caleb in his wheelchair and loaded him into the transport van to gain another neurologist's opinion.

While waiting for a not uncommon hour and a half to see the specialist, Caleb asked every fifteen minutes when we'd be able to see the doctor. That provided a lot of time to come up with creative answers to redirect the thoughts of an impatient patient. After having heard both these songs earlier, I probably should've just busted out singing, "Strength will come." We would have either had a laugh as we waited or been ushered in to see the doctor sooner. We finally welcomed the neurologist's news that there was no need to insert a shunt to relieve the pressure the physicians thought might be pressing on Caleb's brain.

Waiting is such a big part of life, and we considered ours today such an inconvenience. The only way to understand waiting is from the perspective of God. Leaning on the truths of the Bible, we prayed to believe the verse in Isaiah 40:31 (KJV): "But they that wait upon the LORD shall renew their strength...," and to live Psalm 37:7 (NLT): "Be still in the presence of the LORD, and wait patiently for him to act..."

26

CALEB PRAYS AND TESTIFIES

As Caleb's state of confusion was showing no signs of improvement, the doctors were determined to answer all their questions. A sleep study was scheduled during the day to detect any seizure activity that might be occurring. It seemed like all tests continued to come back negative, and though a negative was a positive in Caleb's case, we were still no closer to a medical explanation. We weren't sure if all sleep study labs were the same, but the mattresses in this one were exceptionally nice. It was also a really good thing that Cabe couldn't remember its quality compared to his thin plastic mattress upstairs.

The purpose of the study was to measure the electrical activity across his brain and to identify any abnormalities. Sixteen electrodes were strategically taped to his head for eight hours, and he was asked to try to sleep, or at least to remain perfectly *still*. It was in the stillness and darkness of this room where we heard Caleb pray a prayer that was so beautiful and heart-wrenching; we wanted to keep it forever. With technicians monitoring and recording all activities, it didn't seem to be a problem retrieving a recording at a later time.

Kurt began praying aloud for Caleb, and when he paused to say amen, Caleb followed compellingly with his own prayer. In absolute anguish, Caleb confessed to God that this suffering was so hard, and that he knew God understood because His Son had suffered also. He said he wasn't comparing himself to Jesus but was only acknowledging that God knew what he was going through. As he endured the agony of opening himself up, we were emotionally moved to tears.

Drained, he rested and then asked the question we had answered countless times before: "Where am I?" Not trusting our response that he was in a sleep study lab at TIRR Memorial Hermann Hospital in Houston, Texas, he demanded proof. Nurse Kelly came bursting in from the other room seconds later, solely focused on showing Caleb her ID tag and TIRR embroidered shirt.

Now convinced, his mind *clearly* engaged her in conversation, saying, "This is not a battle like this," and he waved his fists as if punching a bag. "This is a spiritual battle." We believe Cabe's lucid awareness came from the considerable amount time he spent being still and in prayer while not sleeping. We gave thanks for a good day spent with our son—and for a nurse who said she now knew exactly why she'd left the Midwest to come to Texas.

Today was another of our best days. It wasn't because of anything any doctor said. It wasn't because of the right meds. It wasn't because of an accomplishment that Caleb had made. Kurt summed it up well, saying, "I guess the way Caleb helped me today is in how he could testify despite what he is going through, loving God and giving Him the glory and praise. This is the closest thing I've ever seen to a 'Job moment.'" The psalmist said, "My comfort in my suffering is this: Your promise preserves my life" (Psalm 119:50 NIV).

We also agreed wholeheartedly with Abby, who had earlier said, "Now I have seen what it looks like to have God's Word written on your heart."

27

IT'S NOT ABOUT CALEB

"It's not about Caleb" has been an underlying theme revealed to us through the experiences shared by others.

This particular day in March was certainly more about Sarah Kate than Caleb. She was seven, and that number in the Bible is a special number. We took time out from our now normal routine to buy her a birthday present and celebrate in Caleb's room with pizza, cupcakes, and ice cream. Mimi and Uncle Kim also joined the celebration in the hospital room after their long trek from Dallas to see Caleb, and to be with Sarah on her special day. The party then moved to the Wedgeworth's.

SK was treated to her second party with seven cupcakes, 7UP, seven candles, and seven presents. There were even seven people, including her. With all we were experiencing, day in and day out, it was wonderful to have a reason to stop and celebrate. Upon returning to Caleb's room, he especially enjoyed the additional ice cream and asked for more of the leftover cookies. Kurt pulled out the bargaining chip and said one cookie required one lap of assisted walking around the sixth floor. When Caleb requested more ice cream to go with his cookie, the stakes got higher. He made the two additional supported laps with Kurt and then ate half his ice cream before putting us through a workout of our own. It was his line of questioning that mentally drained us.

Caleb asked us to confirm that he was living in a dream. We would not give him this confirmation, fearing it might be harmful to his recovery. When we didn't, he responded in frustration, lashing out at us both physically and verbally. Though not the most extreme aggressive behavior he'd exhibited, it was emotionally painful to take, while still believing that we were helping him the most.

By midnight we resolved to redirect his thoughts and then pick up a similar conversation the next day, knowing he wouldn't remember what he'd put us through the night before. We were in a spirit of despair, and it was evident in our March 11 blog post that we had hit a low point. Within the update it read: "We requested prayer for ourselves and would not have predicted the answer we would receive."

28

MOVING DAY

While Sarah Kate, other family members, and some of Caleb's therapists enjoyed their time away for spring break, Caleb also made a break. We hadn't planned to move Caleb today, and it had never been the plan to move him to Touchstone Neurorecovery Center in Conroe, Texas when we did. In fact, nothing was working out as we had strategically planned, and I now wore the label "Not a Happy Camper." It was a quick decision to move Caleb from TIRR, and it was a forced move. As Jerome described to Kurt, "There's just a big elephant in Caleb's room right now, and we believe Touchstone is the best place to deal with the neurological side of rehab."

I had recently spoken with a representative from Touchstone but hadn't studied the resource materials they offered or been there to check out their facility as we'd done with our preferred option. At this point we had no other alternative, because our first choice wouldn't take a patient who exhibited aggressive behaviors. That left Caleb out.

Caleb displayed his own displeasure at the move as his precious caregiver attempted to settle him into his wheelchair before making our way to the waiting van. After raising his fist backward and soundly hitting Markisha's face, I quickly scolded him as I had when he'd misbehaved as a young boy. My heart absolutely broke, and the gentle tears of sadness turned to harsh tears of pain. This was unbearable. I implored Caleb to apologize, and he simply responded, "That's what she gets for being in my dreams."

The transport van from Touchstone arrived with their own caregivers, and they waited patiently for us to once again say good-bye to those we had come to love so dearly. TIRR's staff and their ministry to us had allowed our family to walk through a tough valley and find ourselves still standing, though weak-kneed. I boarded the van with my purse on my shoulder, while Patrick secured Caleb and his wheelchair by making sure the brake was on, latching buckles at various angles, and tightening the straps so any movement was minimal. I don't really know what Patrick thought, but I wondered if he was more afraid of Caleb with all his aggressions or Caleb's emotional, basket-case mom.

The hour-long trip from downtown Houston to the facility outside Conroe fortunately passed without interruptions. We passed many familiar areas along Interstate 45 North until we exited onto the tollway, taking us away from traffic. With less to pay attention to on the tollway, it was possibly the boredom that brought on the hunger call. Caleb started asking for the snack and drink he was accustomed to having at his immediate disposal between meals, while resting in his room. I was unprepared. All we had done was quickly pack his few belongings and send what snacks we had with Kurt, who was following behind us in our car. What happened next should have been my first clue that provisions were in place where we were heading, but I didn't make the connection at the time.

As Patrick continually asked if we were okay, he heard Caleb's request and instantly pulled a Twinkie and bottled water from his backpack. He was prepared, and both Caleb and I were thankful, for different reasons. A Twinkie and water had saved us from a possible confrontation on the highway. Caleb ate the snack as we merged from the toll road onto the interstate again. Our final exit took us off the busy interstate, heading west now on a farm-to-market road lined with pine trees, toward the recovery center.

We drove onto the peaceful grounds of twenty-five-plus acres and unloaded from the van. Several women took us into a large, well-decorated multi-purpose room where our family was introduced to another new transition team. Patrick then wheeled an agreeable Caleb past the pond to view his new home and private bedroom so Kurt and I could meet with the team uninterrupted.

In a room with four important-looking people and a nurse on speakerphone, Caleb's intake began, and we were asked to share our expectations for his recovery. It didn't take too long to realize that their expectations and ours were at opposite ends of the spectrum concerning our goals for Caleb. While they were wiser in knowing that we needed to look at shorter-term goals, we proceeded to tell them our plans for college reentry in the fall of 2012, now only five and a half months away. We didn't consider the smaller, more important things—like Caleb dressing and feeding himself, walking independently, caring for his personal hygiene, or navigating a simple day's routine. We just thought those were understood, or maybe we just overlooked them.

As they pulled in the reins on our expectations, I pulled in the opposite direction and resolved that I hated this place passionately and that we weren't supposed to be here. My mental aggression was as volatile as Caleb's physical aggression had been only hours earlier.

Our meeting was abruptly interrupted when Patrick reappeared in the room with Caleb. They both had a calm appearance, as Caleb had convinced Patrick that he just wanted the security of seeing his parents. Not only had Caleb eaten more of Patrick's snack stash, he had abused his trust. Caleb's true motivation was to get back to us and then inform us—that *he did not want to be here*! He was very angry, screaming confidently as he flailed his arms wildly to illustrate that there was definitely nothing *wrong* with him!

As Kurt knelt in front of Caleb's wheelchair and ever so calmly disagreed, Caleb reached out, forcibly grabbed Kurt by the neck, and shook him violently with both hands. I guess we could've never described to this group the "elephant in the room" more graphically than Caleb was able to display it. But regardless, I wanted the elephant gone, and I wanted to know how they planned to do it.

The staff had complete faith in the founder of Touchstone Neurorecovery Center, Dr. John W. Cassidy, whose expertise is respected and proven in the field relating to brain injuries. Our minimal inquiries about Dr. Cassidy unveiled that it was not the norm for him to oversee individual patients at Touchstone but rather to delegate patients to his neurology staff. We believed his interest in Caleb was in our favor, and it also confirmed the severity of Caleb's injury. The meeting ended with plans in place, though I'm not sure I knew what they were.

We moved Caleb into Windsor House, one of the four Touchstone homes, and unpacked him for his first night's stay. As I recall, I didn't like anything I saw other than his room. (To be fair, there was nothing anyone could've shown me that would have been satisfactory to me at this point.) I did like the bedroom setting, since it didn't resemble a hospital room. There was no net bed, and the furnishings seemed fitting for a college dorm room, though I would've chosen a more modern comforter.

Fears set in early, and I feared that Caleb would fall from his bed and bump his head on the bedside table close at hand or on the tiled floor just a few feet away. His one-to-one caregiver, who sat in a chair eight feet from his bed, was to keep close watch on him at all times, twenty-four-seven, as had been the case for the past three and a half months. I wanted a monitor to monitor his monitor. My trust was failing.

29

HOME AWAY FROM HOME

My misjudgments began from the start, as I believed these people were incapable of caring for Caleb as he needed to be cared for. I also had fears about other residents and their freedoms and behaviors in this home setting. Windsor House was the entry-level home for the most injured residents, and it was set up much like any home.

After ringing the doorbell and entering through the secured front door, one could see a large living area directly opposite a large kitchen and dining area. The differences were the additional small conference room to the left in the entry way, and the offices and nurse's station straight ahead. Down multiple hallways were bedrooms set up somewhat like a dorm, with a half-bath shared between two individual rooms. The hallways were wider than an average home to accommodate the passing of wheelchairs going to and from the showers set on either side of the house.

Patients at Touchstone were there from all over the United States to be cared for while recovering from brain injuries, either from accidents or medical-related conditions. Some residents were very loud and very verbal, and some were silent. Some had been there for only months, while others had been there for years, if not permanently. Their ages spanned from teenagers to the elderly. Most had behavior issues resulting from this insidious injury, and all were trying to rehab to the point of living independently.

I felt uncomfortable in this setting, and it reminded Kurt of the Oscar-winning film, *One Flew Over the Cuckoo's Nest*—absent Nurse Ratched. We found ourselves in a quandary and didn't want to be in this movie. Unfortunately, we soberly thought, Caleb had just satisfied the audition requirements to be here.

Sadly, I had reached another low and had used poor judgment in almost everything. To trust God at this moment seemed beyond my capabilities, and as Kurt and I drove away that night, I told him, "This is the worst night of my life." I felt like I was betraying Caleb, and joy was nowhere to be found by me. I was mad at Kurt; I was mad at God; and I was content just to be mad. I honestly wanted to know just what was wrong with the way I had things planned in my head—again.

Sometimes we don't receive specific answers other than, "Trust Me," and that was specific enough, considering the source. Being mad and trusting work against each other. My negative was driving me away from the positive coming my direction. Kurt was hurting from having to leave Caleb, and he also felt the burden of not being able to fix my hurt. It was a heavy load for any man to carry.

What a blessing it turned out to be when I was leaving Caleb's new home the next day and he didn't ask me to take him with me. He only asked if he would see me tomorrow.

Since Kurt had to be away from us for the *first* time for a set work commitment, I was flying solo when I arrived to see Caleb. The closer the time inched toward our visit, the more anxious I felt. I was so frightened of the circumstances. The load lightened as I walked through the secured front door and was met with good reports regarding Caleb's day. He had been restful for most of it and hadn't been aggressive toward his caregivers.

When I entered his room, his first request was a hug, and with that embrace, he cried. He asked me to pray over him many times, and doing so was healing for both of us. He agreed to let me take him outside after multiple offerings of a bribe, with his snack finally tilting the scale. At one point Caleb looked at me ever so intently and commented, "I just want to look at you so I can remember you in my dreams." How nice that felt, as I immediately also thought about Jesus and how He too wants us to look ever so intently at Him—lest we forget.

As the time neared to leave that evening, I signed the journal, reminding Caleb that we had been there each day and we were sure to return tomorrow. I thought, *God left us a book, signed by Himself, promising He too would return to us and someday take us home.* From one of the shakiest mornings of my life, I had been lifted to the point of being able to hug Caleb, tell him good night, and walk to the front door without a teardrop.

As I reached for the doorknob, Caleb's relayed message came for one more hug and the reassurance I would return. I gladly hugged him and gave him the assurance that he needed, just as my Father had done for me this evening.

The following day, I was ever so thankful to have Kurt back. We had an anxious meeting of the minds with Dr. Cassidy and his team of experts for the first time. He was resolute in telling us he'd seen patients such as Caleb rehabilitated, but he gave us no guarantees, even if he is a leading national expert in the field of neurosciences and behavioral disorders. He had reviewed all previous medical records, and validated that Caleb had suffered a very severe traumatic brain injury. He informed us for any meaningful rehabilitation to occur, Caleb's hallmark point of recovery would be clearing his post-traumatic amnesia, coupled with treating his current behavior in the meantime.

While he attested to seeing cases like Caleb's in the past thirty years, he could not "come down the mountain carrying tablets carved in stone." Just hearing him use words referring to Moses in the Bible relaxed both Kurt and me and opened the door to share our son's faith, giving the team a glimpse of who truly held Caleb's heart. We encouraged them to pray with him and for him, and we assured them that they too were being prayed for (despite our feelings over the last forty-eight hours). It was an opportunity to refocus our attention on the one who etched the commandments in stone, not on the stone carrier. After our meeting, we were able to give thanks and then visit Caleb after his nearly full day of sleeping. Since Caleb had been "up and at 'em" pretty much every day at TIRR, whether he wanted to or not, we were disappointed to hear that he'd been resting all day again. It was good news, just not what we were hoping for.

The week had flown by quickly since Sarah's birthday celebration when we arrived at Windsor House for lunch on an early spring Saturday. We were pleased to see that Caleb had gotten up and eaten breakfast after an assisted shower. We had brought him lunch, and during our conversation, the question as to where he was now arose. It had taken six weeks of everyone at TIRR asking him daily if he knew where he was, before he'd finally been able to tell us he was at TIRR. The one thing Caleb *did* know now was that he was no longer at TIRR, and he expressed being afraid. That only fed my own personal fears, and when returning to his room I gladly read, at his request, from the *Jesus Calling* sitting at his bedside.

Our fears diminished with each word I spoke: "Come to Me for understanding, since I know you far better than you know yourself. I comprehend you in all of your complexity; no detail of your life is hidden from me." As I was reading, Kurt was scratching Caleb's back and calming him. Our Father was relaxing us both, and the picture on my camera phone minutes later captured it all: Kurt and Caleb lay on his twin bed, hand in hand, both sleeping peacefully.

30

VANILLA SHAKE, ANYONE?

Sadly, the peace didn't last the whole day. We took a break while Caleb rested some more, and returned during the evening, bearing a gift of a vanilla milk shake. We still seemed to be in the ice cream delivery business—thanks to merchant's gift cards from some generous friends. It was our tool to persuade Caleb to leave the comfort of his room, mostly by wheelchair, and enjoy the surroundings of the outdoor acreage the four homes sat on.

Touchstone is a peaceful setting—except for a shooting range sitting directly across the highway behind a dense line of pine trees. Though our eyes could not see it from where we sat, the noises coming through the tree line were not secure. Caleb didn't seem to notice as much as we did. He was more focused now on begging and pleading for us to take him with us. If he could've read my thoughts, he would have known how great my temptation was to push him back inside, pack his personal things, and head south to our real home. Fortunately for everyone, I didn't try to act on my thoughts. Instead we tried our best to remind him why he was here and to convince him that this was the best place for him.

As on previous occasions when we told him no, he quickly became agitated. We realized our visit wasn't valuable to Caleb after his half hour of constant pleading to our dissatisfying answers, so we thought it best to try to redirect his thoughts and take him back to his room. Kurt handed Caleb the milk shake for one last sip, and that's when Caleb took the opportunity to share it with Kurt.

After Caleb's quick, well-aimed toss and Kurt's not-so-quick block, they were both wearing the vanilla shake. Kurt calmly wiped the excess from both of them as we moved toward the Windsor House. It helped me to see how short-lived these focused outbursts were. Caleb had almost immediately settled down, and Kurt was able to shave him and help him into the security of his bed before we left.

Though things were more peaceful at the moment, it remained difficult to walk out the front door and leave him.

SECOND CHANCES

The psalmist said, "The LORD is merciful and compassionate, slow to get angry and filled with unfailing love" (Psalm 145:8 NLT). Today I witnessed Caleb's earthly father giving him a second chance. Kurt didn't walk in with just a vanilla milk shake this time but with a "Blast" containing Oreos. Caleb didn't remember the milk shake from the day before—or "sharing" it. He silently stared at the spoon, focusing on each bite as he moved it slowly and deliberately from the cup to his waiting, open mouth, sharing minimal bites with his dad. Once again Kurt and Caleb both had ice cream on their shirts, but fortunately it was only from the drippings off the spoon. We were thankful that this day came without incident.

We were reminded of all the provisions God had given us in abundance, and those that He would continue to give. We were sad to officially leave the beautiful home in Houston where we had been made to feel so at-home. Initially Sarah Kate didn't approve of the move, even though our newly provided home sat on beautiful Lake Conroe only eight miles from Touchstone versus an hour commute from downtown Houston. The welcome at my sister-in-love's mother's lake house furnished a large-mouth bass that Kurt and Sarah caught from the pier, and the comfort I experienced from seeing three devotional books lying on the table: *Jesus Calling*, *Dear Jesus*, and *Nearer to Jesus*, all by Sarah Young.

A Christian radio station had also unknowingly sent a message as we made our way north only a mile from the Wedgeworths' home. I sang with the song in my cracking voice: "Where you go, I'll go. Where you stay, I'll stay. When you move, I'll move. I will follow." I was thankful to the messenger of that song, even if it didn't bring me pleasure.

We unpacked the cars in disbelief at how much we had again accumulated on top of our Colorado accumulation and then made our way to Touchstone to be with Cabe. He had a better day, in spite of still being aggravated at our not taking him with us. We met Emma for the first time as she was serving as Caleb's caregiver for the day. She had just finished reading *Jesus Calling* and praying with him. She spoke a blessing and reassured us when she said, "God has Caleb in His hands."

As a full afternoon approached evening, Caleb's countenance was very loving, and he hugged us good-bye many times. He thanked us for the Blast, which was becoming a daily ritual, and hugged us one last time. We then took off for Baytown to pick up Sarah Kate, who was finishing spring break with her grandparents. She met us, jumped into our arms, and asked, "Does Caleb still feel like he's dreaming?"

A week is a very long time for a seven-year-old, and she hoped we would answer no. With disappointment, we answered, "Yes, he does." But we continued to hope for the day when we'd say, "Not anymore!" We loaded up all her clothes and stuffed animals and moved her once again.

32

EXPECT DELAYS

We were really excited to see how Caleb would respond to seeing his sister after being apart for over a week. We weren't excited about his actual response—in fact, it saddened and hurt us all deeply. Caleb became agitated with Sarah's questions and curiosity as she went about observing his new living quarters for the first time. After listening to a seven-year-old's endless account of the new surroundings, his final comment to her was, "Shut … up," accompanied with profanity highly unlikely to ever roll off Caleb's tongue.

It blew the sticks-and-stones saying right out the window. The tongue can be heart-crushing! Not only was Sarah Kate devastated, but Kurt and I were as well. Evening came and we left Caleb ready for bed, trying our best to understand that he would've *never* said those words to Sarah Kate before his accident. Fortunately for Caleb, he wouldn't remember saying those words when he saw us the next day. I only wished we could erase them from our memories as well.

After leaving Touchstone we sat silently in a long line of traffic on the loop, staring at a lighted sign ahead. Kurt and I both took the message personally as the words slowly came into focus. The blinking lights said, "Expect Delays." Traffic was being slowed because of a convoluted mess of roadwork construction ahead of us. It was necessary work for improved traffic flow, but navigating through bumper-to-bumper traffic and lane changes to arrive at our destination required us to patiently wait in the meantime. It was similar to where we found ourselves in the construct of Caleb's healing. We had to remind ourselves that while sitting on this road to recovery wouldn't be forever, we were getting to know better the One who was healing Caleb—in the meantime. The sign also flashed His plans might be larger, and that progress might come at a much slower pace than we hoped. After all, none of us likes traffic delays—or life delays.

We were given a reminder from Oswald Chamber's writings concerning Abraham being asked to leave Ur without details for the journey. "By faith Abraham went, even though he did not know where he was headed. Living a life of faith means never knowing where you are being led. But it does mean loving and knowing the ONE who is leading. It is a life of faith, not of understanding and reason: A life of knowing Him who calls us to go."

I clearly understood why God wouldn't give Abraham the details of where he was going and all that would take place. Abraham possibly would have rejected the plan and missed the blessing. I felt confident God knew what He was doing in the life of Abraham because I knew the whole story.

The trouble came in transferring the lesson of this particular devotion to my own life and circumstances. We were clearly being called to move in faith without knowing the plan. We were relying on the same God who had called Abraham to move, and we would put our trust in Him despite the delays. He had a sign flashing right before our opened eyes to reveal that to us: "Expect Delays."

33

IT'S STILL RAINING...

The words of a song sung by Casting Crowns starts out saying exactly what we were thinking: "I was sure by now you would have reached down and wiped our tears away; stepped in and saved the day." Yet the songwriter conveys that it continues to rain and the thunder rolls.

The cold rain blew across Lake Conroe as a three-foot blue heron stood motionless atop the semi-circular awning serving as the jet ski's boathouse. I thought of Caleb as I watched the bird nervously begin to pace back and forth across its rounded peak, stopping only momentarily to try to stretch her long neck and wings to catch flight. Battered and unsure, the bird would quickly pull her large wings back into the safety of her body, only to try again after each of her numerous attempts.

Finally retreating to the safety of the dock's lower level, she found shelter from the strong wind by the same canvas that had presented her with problems above. Now in a safe place, she stably spread her wings before taking off into the brisk north wind, successfully flying low across the water to her next destination.

Caleb's view was much the same. He still remained on the familiar canvas of post-traumatic amnesia (PTA), considered the dream state. And even though continually reminded of his safety and protection, he still didn't remember what he'd been told or had experienced two minutes earlier. He wasn't ready to spread his wings into this storm, no matter how much anyone would like him to!

The brain is incredibly amazing. It can consciously tell you your broken arm is still healing when you see your cast, or to release the handle of a cast-iron frying pan when it becomes too hot. But the brain cannot tell you when it has been injured. It cannot feel pain. For Caleb, the current flight plan just didn't make sense, and it wouldn't until his episodic memory—the ability to remember what he'd had for breakfast or the attached sensation with whomever he had seen the day before—started to return. These hallmark moments would be the beginning of the end of his post-traumatic amnesia—and the beginning of his meaningful recovery.

In the meantime, we listened for the still, small voice that echoed in the remainder of the song. It continued: "As the thunder rolls, I barely hear you whisper through the rain, 'I'm with you.'" The chorus sums up the song, saying, "No matter where I am in the storms of this life, I will praise the God who gives and takes away." The songwriter was honest enough to say that even with a heart that was torn, he would still praise God in the storm.

Kurt and I have had the privilege of participating in and facilitating a discipleship course called *Experiencing God* by Henry Blackaby for many years. We both embrace the teaching from the Bible story about the disciples and Jesus in a boat. A huge storm came upon the fishermen on the Sea of Galilee, and waves poured into their boat, threatening to sink it. Jesus was in the stern, sleeping, and was awakened by the disciples asking Him why He didn't care that they were sinking. Jesus told the wind to pipe down and instructed the sea to settle down. At His word, the wind ran out of breath, and the sea became as smooth as glass. He then reprimanded the disciples for their lack of faith.

As we have found ourselves in situations where we felt sure that sinking was imminent, we've borrowed the phrase we learned in our study: "Truth is in the boat." With Jesus in the boat, the circumstances have no power. He but says the word, and they are quiet. We asked the many who were faithfully following the CaringBridge posts to pray we would have a strong, un-cowardly faith in the midst of this storm, and to give thanks for the rain. We were in need of help.

TIRED BUT RENEWED

I chose my own delay this morning. I stayed in bed to avoid facing the day. When I finally did drag myself into the den area, Kurt confessed that he too was tired and desired for this part of the journey to be over. We found strength and support in each other as we talked. We were encouraged by notes on CaringBridge, texts from friends, the *Jesus Calling* devotional, and the beautiful sun shining over the lake, which was a contrast from the day before. We knew that God was speaking to us in many ways to stir us to stay the course.

We toured parts of the Touchstone facility we hadn't seen in our sudden move, and were able to visit with the staff neuropsychologist, from whom we gained much knowledge. We were also informed that Caleb had gotten up this morning and eaten four bowls of cereal, been pushed in his wheelchair around the pond, had agreed to have a caregiver read him scripture as an activity, and participated in a group session late into the afternoon. He had shown little agitation and aggression this day. Instead of his usual request for us to take him home with us, he opted to sleep. Caleb was visibly tired from the day's activities, and his concerned caregiver felt bad that he was sleeping during our visit. We assured Theresa we were happy to see Caleb, whether he was sleeping or awake.

At the end of this day, we noted in Caleb's journal that this had been by far his best day yet at Touchstone, and we thanked God for giving him a full and productive one! We also rejoiced after downloading a new song Theresa recalled hearing recently. We too agreed with the lyrics and could say, "We are alive—when the hurt and the healer collide!"

GOD-WINKS AND CONNECTORS

The days became long, and Caleb's progress seemed slow and even nonexistent at times. I refused to believe his healing had come to a halt, but I wasn't seeing evidence of it. During these especially hard times (which we had both already experienced and wouldn't stop anytime in the near future), friends prayed Kurt and I would see the "God-winks" that meant so much.

While restocking our needs in Walmart, a precious friend (much younger than I) called to tell me that she now lived in Conroe and would help in any way I needed. It turned out Chrissie lived only five minutes from Touchstone and would be a safe haven for Sarah Kate to spend some much-needed time of normalcy while we were with Caleb. SK's time was monopolized with good care, and Monopoly became her new game of choice: a wink and a divine provision for sure.

God also revealed that He was connecting his own people united through Caleb's injury. My BFF in Dallas shared her prayer requests for Caleb, and a woman came to her immediately following Sunday school to say that she was already praying. She is the mother of one of Caleb's best Aggie friends connected through the Baptist Student Ministry in College Station. Both were already praying in very personal ways, and this revelation encouraged us. These two connections were certainly enough assurance of things we hoped for, but God chose to give us more to see. It's as if He was saying, "Focus on My eyes, because I am going to wink at you really big."

Hunter was on a mission trip in Haiti over spring break, as were many other volunteers after a hurricane ravaged this country. He was a student at Oklahoma State University, and had served closely with Caleb at iGo Global Ministries during previous summer months. The needs in Haiti were dire, and Hunter soon found himself helping a small boy who had fallen and hurt his leg. Trying to console the boy, Hunter took him to a different group of volunteers and to a man who possessed medical supplies.

Juri and Hunter were attending to the needs of the young boy, when the maroon bracelet bearing "Caleb Jentsch" on one side and "Nahum 1:7" on the other side stood out. Juri had been a nurse in Denver's trauma ICU unit who professed Jesus as his Lord. He had played worship music in Caleb's room, and ministered to us through prayer and encouragement. Their meeting in Haiti blew me away. The fact that these two men would meet in the midst of the Haitians while serving as volunteers on the same square yard of ground—and became aware that they both knew Caleb—was truly unbelievable to me. I realized all the circumstances had to be just right to make that moment happen, and could have only been coordinated by God. I also understood God is always up to kingdom work, and I couldn't make judgments about the work taking place based on what I was or was not seeing in Caleb.

The smile was the final gift on this day. I prayed while driving to Touchstone to just see Caleb smile, since I hadn't witnessed one from him in quite a while. Upon walking into Touchstone with his aunt, uncle, and cousin, we were told Caleb was eating dinner and had become quite angry after being awakened from a long nap. It was these special visitors who brought a brief smile to his face, and as he enjoyed their gift of cheesecake, I savored the smile.

Just as God had provided me with more, they provided Caleb with more. They scratched his back and rubbed his feet. He was loved, and the many people connections continued to show evidence of the tie that binds us together.

CARRYING AND PRAYING

In the Bible is the story of a paralyzed man who was carried by four friends onto a rooftop and then lowered through a hole to where Jesus was sitting so He could heal him. Caleb's wheelchair still served as his carrier of choice to move him from place to place at Touchstone when four college friends came to visit on March 27.

Caleb wasn't much in the visiting mood when they arrived, and most of the conversation was between his friends and me. He did smile upon seeing them, and then slept through nearly all the rest of their stay. When his friends did get the chance to ask him how they could pray, Caleb urged them to pray for his dreams, because some were filled with sharks and were pretty scary. At my suggestion, he agreed we should also pray for him to walk and not be as dependent on his wheelchair—just as many other students had assembled to pray specifically for him the night before.

At the end of the next day our attempts to wake Caleb proved unsuccessful, because he was literally spent after participating in a full day of therapies. We had experienced the "yes" answer to our prayer requests. We knew that the group of students who continued to meet on Monday nights to pray for Caleb were the faithful ones carrying him against all obstacles and placing him at the feet of Jesus, the Healer. We boldly asked others to pray for Caleb to walk and for his brain to be completely healed, above and beyond what could ever be imagined, so we could all declare, "Praise God! We have never seen anything like this before."

We prayed the model prayer that Jesus prayed: "Our Father in heaven, may your name be kept holy. May your Kingdom come soon. May your will be done on earth, as it is in heaven. Give us today what we need, and forgive us our sins, As we have forgiven those who sin against us. And don't let us yield to temptation but rescue us from the evil one. For thine is the kingdom, the power, and the glory forever. Amen" (Matthew 6:9-13 NLT; KJV).

When Caleb couldn't be awakened from a heavy sleep, we were both glad and sad. Our gladness was in response to Caleb's efforts on this day. Our sadness was due to the fact that Kurt was leaving for home the next day, and physically returning to work after the Frost family had allowed us to be by each other's side for the last eighty-two days. Caleb didn't hear his dad say, "Good-bye, son. I love you." But he would read the words in his daily journal along with the words, "I'll be back in a few days." It was no surprise; I cried.

YOU ARE ON THE MIND OF GOD

In recent days I'd asked God to give me a surety of things hoped for. Over the course of a few days, He spoke through other believers to do just that. I received an encouraging e-mail from a pastor/friend I knew from college days, a personal phone call from a trusted friend sharing her experiences of God's healing power, and a missed phone call from a well-known Bible teacher who authored the study our women's group finished just before Christmas. I felt like I knew this author personally because she had taught me from the pages of my book and from the big-screen television in my den.

Most women who participate in a Priscilla Shirer study feel the same way about this kindred spirit. The call showed up on my cell phone as "unknown," and it's not my habit to take such calls. So, when the call went to voice mail, I was humbly surprised as I listened to the message she left. *Maybe I should have taken that call*, I thought as I walked into the room where my beloved friend from Victoria sat.

With tear-stained cheeks, I told her she wouldn't believe what I'd just heard. As Priscilla introduced herself (like I didn't recognize her voice!), she told me how she had become aware of our circumstances and been led to pray for us. "Ms. Deborah," she said, "I want you to know you are on the mind of God." That still make my eyes well up. Being on the mind of God is so beyond what I could comprehend. I took comfort in those words, knowing they were the Truth and were directly related to my feeble prayer for reassurance. I needed to remember them for many hard days ahead, and I would have her message to remind me over and over again. I also feel certain that had I answered, Priscilla might never have spoken this message to me for the sake of my babbling.

The truth she shared with me is confirmed by the Psalm: "How precious are your thoughts about me, O God. They cannot be numbered! I can't even count them; they outnumber the grains of sand! And when I wake, up you are still with me!" (Psalm 139:17–18 NLT).

As evening approached, my parents visited Caleb for the first time since we'd moved to Touchstone. It was a hard visit for them, and one I can relate to well, recalling my own feelings the first time I arrived. We sat with Cabe as he ate dinner, and then Granddaddy pushed him around the grounds several times before ending up back in his room. Caleb quickly became fixated on sleeping, but didn't refuse a foot rub and a brief conversation with Grandmother once he settled into bed. He repeated her words at her request, "I will get better," as well as Granddaddy's, "You are special," a phrase they shared when Caleb was four years old. Granddaddy would often ask Caleb, "Why are you so special?" And without missing a beat Caleb would reply, "Because God made me that way!"

Thank goodness for these truths spoken to me today, to have and hold against the circumstances when discerning the tomorrows.

In a world that "does" and "goes," I was disappointed to hear that Caleb hadn't done anything or gone anywhere during the day. He had missed all of his therapies. I would need to remember I had not left the mind of God. I would also need to be reminded God does not sleep or slumber.

38

MAD ... YET AMAZED

I was frustrated by Caleb's lack of activity, but before I allowed myself to become mad, I turned to my source of help: Kurt. I was looking for someone to blame and direct my anger toward, and I felt sure that he could help me determine who needed to be straightened out. The only problem was—he didn't totally agree with me.

Instead he tried to help me calm down, encouraging me to go back to the One we trust. I slept peacefully that night after reading the scripture telling me, "He will not let your foot slip—he who watches over Israel will neither slumber nor sleep" (Psalm 121:3–4 NIV).

Starting off my next morning with my usual habit, I read *Jesus Calling* for the day. It was titled "Stop Trying to Work Things Out." I had already been told (and reminded) that God was in control, so I have no idea why I would be so stupid as to take control by walking into Touchstone to try to fix things. It hadn't worked out in my favor previously, and I was in need of confession and repentance.

I prayed to remember January 5, when God answered my prayer, saying, "Yes, Caleb will have life," and God's answer on January 6, when his oxygen levels rose above 21, and then the gift of Caleb's responsiveness on my birthday. Day 13 was when Caleb had opened his eyes. God had not slept. I was the sleeping one, drifting into a slumber away from Him. It was on this last day of March when we stopped and took time to count the many blessings Caleb still retained, like seeing, hearing, smelling, feeling, and his ability to remember through long-term memory. As stated by Sarah Young, "Understanding will fail you" (as it had failed me this week), "but trust will keep you close to Me" (as it did when we counted our blessings).

Dr. Cassidy was also able to help us manage our anxiousness by bringing clarity to what we didn't understand. Caleb continued to be held captive in post-traumatic amnesia by his injury, which most patients would have started to clear by now. He explained that a biological healing in Caleb's brain needed to take place, and *nothing* we tried to do would hurry that process. I was in a hurry, but God was revealing He was not. After all, if He was, we would be in a different place, and He would have a plan different from Touchstone, right?

I began to think about what happens when we are in a hurry, either individually or corporately: mistakes are made, and we skip things. There is disorder, and others are trampled on. The truth of the matter is, "Peace trumps hurry," and is best played if we will just trust Him and rest in it. In John 20:19 Jesus' first words to His huddled-up disciples were for their greatest need following His resurrection, as they feared for their lives and He needed to clear their thinking, "Peace be with you!" No doubt, He was here with Caleb and us too, and His assurance became very evident to us as we approached the Windsor House on that first Sunday afternoon of April.

The joyful news came through Caleb's caregivers. The first thrilling report was that he'd been on the back porch for much of the morning talking and interacting with them and other residents. And when the newest Windsor resident randomly began singing, "His Eye Is on the Sparrow," Caleb almost immediately joined in to complete a beautiful duet—much to the staff's amazement.

Tuckered out from the day's mental activity, our family time outside was cut in half when Caleb asked to go inside and get into bed. Kurt assisted him with a shower and shave and then helped him dress. Hugs, prayers, and journal signing completed, Caleb was quickly sound asleep, and we were headed toward the front door. Reaching to grab the doorknob, we were stopped to be introduced to the young brain-injured man Caleb had accompanied in singing. He willingly and graciously sang the morning's reprise for all the residents still up watching TV.

It was so inspiring to hear him sing the words, "I sing because I'm happy, I sing because I'm free." In this house of recovery, where he wasn't allowed to leave, he could still sing of his freedom in God. As SK pushed the security button and we were exiting Windsor House, we heard the young man's excited voice quicken and grow louder, repeating, "Something is going on around here. Something is going on here!"

Stepping back inside, we all readily agreed. Our eyes focused in on the Country Music Awards on the small TV screen. The song, being sung at that very moment to those tuned in all over the United States was none other than, "His Eye Is on the Sparrow." The professional singers, no doubt, were singing to a much larger audience, but it was the smaller, more intimate one at Touchstone to whom God gave a very special blessing on this night. It was true: "something" was going on around there.

39

TIME FOR SCHOOL

It was a Monday morning, and as on most Mondays, it felt like a blah kind of day. During the wait before our normal evening visit with Caleb, we took care of some personal business and promoted our homeschool assignments with Sarah Kate.

Caleb had displayed agitation throughout the day after requesting to lie down but not being allowed to, per doctor's orders. Strapped into his wheelchair, he was kept from acting on his desire to lie down, so he acted out in aggravation. Our arrival with dinner and dessert seemed timely and helped redirect his thoughts. With redirected thoughts came a more positive attitude.

A quiet meal was followed by an opportunity to walk it off, and Caleb's physical improvement in the motions of walking, minus his balance, was evident to Kurt. So with Dad's support, Caleb agreed to walk around the grounds outside the buildings and then wearily requested to go to his room. We encouraged him to stay in the den, but he'd had enough togetherness. We were thankful for the safety that he now found in what he had accepted as "his" room, even though he still couldn't lead us to it on his own.

Few words were spoken as Cabe slowly settled in for the night, seeming to be in deep thought. Kurt asked him what he was thinking about, and Caleb responded, "I'm just trying to figure out how school is going to work out for me."

I bent down within six inches of Caleb's face, being sure I had his attention, and just grinned. Kurt explained to Caleb that my smile expressed the joy we both felt at the possibility he was beginning to accept what had happened. The verses from this morning's *Jesus Calling* served as the perfect answer to Caleb's question as Kurt read Philippians 4:19 (NIV): "And my God will meet all your needs according to the riches of his glory in Christ Jesus," and 2 Corinthians 4:17 (NIV): "For our light and momentary troubles are achieving for us an eternal glory that far outweighs them all."

40

EASTER APPROACHES

The week leading up to Easter was eventful for Caleb in many ways. The medicine controlling his aggression was cut back to allow him to be less subdued and thereby participate more during therapies. Therapists also decided they'd now start going to Caleb's room when he chose (most of the time) not to go to them. It just seemed better not to raise his anxiety level to a fighting mode, only to transfer him to the therapy building and not be productive.

Unfortunately, his physical therapists didn't get to observe his most accomplished physical movement to date. The report actually came from several caregivers and residents who witnessed Caleb chasing his newly employed one-on-one caregiver out of his room and down the hallway! Her baptism by fire came after she cheerfully and energetically tried to encourage Caleb to leave his bed numerous times to participate in the day's therapies.

The way Kurt and I received what was reported to us was very different. I was personally concerned for this sweet, young caregiver who was fairly new to the job, had never watched Caleb before, and apparently had never gotten his therapists' memo either. She was fearful and in flight mode when Caleb ran after her down the hallway, to the amazement of residents and staff who quickly came to her wide-eyed rescue.

Kurt, on the other hand, though thankful no one was hurt, was equally thankful Caleb had taken the opportunity to demonstrate his physical capabilities. When queried to clarify the word *chased*, the care team said they had engaged a determined Caleb during a "semi-controlled" sprint, not just a fast walk. Wow! We were amazed at the scene, as were many of his eyewitnesses who had cautiously tried their best to intervene.

Caleb's increasing body strength was something to be thankful for, along with his diminishing fears, and the sense that he was sleeping well and not mentioning a dream as often. He was also becoming more aware of any background noise surrounding his space at any particular moment. This was not only Good Friday; it was a good Friday.

The picture on the opening page of our CaringBridge site had been taken on Easter Sunday two years ago. Caleb, then a freshman at A&M, was smiling while displaying one of Sarah's eggs he had retrieved. I couldn't imagine what I would've done had I been given notice of where I would be two years in the future on Easter Sunday. Jesus knew all along where He was headed, and He chose to do it anyway. That's what makes His love so incredible. He *chose* to die for us.

Kurt, Sarah Kate, and I celebrated that love at the sunrise service by the lake, which was followed by her filling a basket with eggs at the community church's annual Easter egg hunt. We then joined others at Touchstone for a delicious Easter meal, along with a side of fried okra that we'd picked up for Caleb, which, honestly, he'd much rather have over Easter candy any day. Kurt and Caleb took another opportunity to walk afterward, stopping to stretch his arm muscles above and behind his head again before making our way back to his room. Stretching his arm still hurt Cabe a little, but he managed the "good" pain without a negative response.

Our Sunday was like many Sundays in our family. We all took an afternoon nap in Caleb's room wherever we found a spot. Caleb got the bed, Sarah Kate curled up on a pallet at the foot of the bed, I sat next to Cabe with my head propped against the wall, and Kurt reclined the best he could in a non-reclining chair. We were together as in Easters past, just in a different location. Kurt testified to the fact that he and Caleb had spent most of the last ninety-three days with each other, and though they had been tough, their consistent times of prayer and words of love during them were probably more than most dads would experience. Just as Caleb had been physically stretched on this Easter Sunday, we were being spiritually stretched with hopes to be strengthened.

41

DEWBERRY PIE

Those of us living in south Texas love dewberries, and we assume the rest of the world does too. It surprises us to know the rest of humanity is missing out on our little wild berries and that some even doubt their delectable existence. They are much like a blackberry, growing wild when the weather conditions have been favorable.

Knowing Caleb was tempted and persuaded with desserts, it came as no surprise that Caleb changed his mind about visiting with our friend from Victoria. He first told me how tired he was after slightly lifting his head and smiling as we came into his room. Upon hearing Lori had brought daughter Ashley's famous dewberry pie, he decided he wasn't too tired to drag himself out of bed and have a piece.

Lori was a good judge of the headway Caleb had made, since she hadn't seen him in a while. She observed that his walking was much stronger and more balanced, and that his ability to independently care for some of his basic needs showed dramatic improvement. We were most thankful for her reports, because we couldn't always fully recognize and appreciate Caleb's improvements while being with him day in and day out. We gave God thanks and praises for allowing us to see the great things He had done through the eyes of others, and Lori ended her visit by praying with Caleb and his caregivers.

Caleb was enjoying the perks of being cared for, and now requested back-scratching and foot rubs nearly every visit. When I told him it was time for me to leave, he pleaded for more. I responded as I would have done with a young child, making it known he only had five more minutes, and then I quickly set the timer on my phone.

On one occasion, he asked to see my phone only to return it back seconds later with the timer reset for an additional twenty. I laughed and actually liked that his processing skills were working well, though primarily in his favor. I too was quickly reminded by a guestbook entry how wonderful it was that Caleb just wanted to spend time with me—more time than I would allow.

I couldn't help but reexamine the time I spend with God as being much like my time with Caleb. I put a limit on it, and once the timer goes off in my head, I am off and moving on to what was next on my agenda. Oh, that I would let Him control the time we spend one-on-one together and just enjoy His company. The hours spent with Caleb each day were allowing us much more time to spend with God to personally seek His help and direction in the days ahead.

Tomorrow we would boast of God's presence during the past one hundred days.

42

100 DAYS

On this hundredth day since Caleb's injury, we remained at Touchstone Neuro Recovery Center in Conroe, Texas, located right off of a two-lane farm-to-market road. I have been to and through Conroe my entire life. My mother spent many of her childhood years here while her daddy worked on the Sinclair Oil pipeline. She lived in a community of houses called a *station*, later called the Silver Star Ranch. When Googling its exact location for our site visit, we learned Silver Star was a mere five miles down the road from Touchstone.

After visiting there years ago, my mother was quoted on the facility's website. She shared her history of being born there and her years as an eight-year-old running and playing on those same grounds. It fascinated me to read about these moments in her life, knowing that God already knew her grandson would be in a nearby facility seventy-three years later, relearning how to walk just as she had first learned to.

We were all learning to walk in different ways, and today we were being taught to walk in the truth of what God says, not what we see and hear. I anxiously anticipated the day when I would walk into Touchstone and hear the words, "Today was a *great* day for Caleb." But it was not today. The minute I entered Windsor's front door, I was greeted by Caleb's caregivers with just the opposite: "It was a tough day for Caleb."

Stirring the memories of my mother's birthplace, I also recalled my grandparents patiently teaching us to play Texas 42, a game of dominoes. It's much like the game of cards called Spades, and whenever a trump is laid down on the table, that domino wins the round, no matter what else has been played. I decided I needed some trump cards of my own for the tough moments when I needed peace, so I wrote Bible verses on index cards (which I had been encouraged to do) to play (read) when necessary.

When Dana reported the news of Caleb's tough day, I chose the trump card that said, "This is the day the LORD has made; let us rejoice and be glad in it" (Psalm 118:24 ESV). When told the medicine added today might cause Caleb to be more unhinged in his awakened state, I used Isaiah's trump card: "He gives strength to the weary and increases the power of the weak" (Isaiah 40:29 NIV). I hoped I'd written out enough cards after hearing that Caleb was unable to participate in therapies today. "Ugh" was my gut response before slamming down 1 Chronicles 16:11 (NIV): "Look to the LORD and his strength; seek his face always!"

With trump cards played, it didn't take long before we *found* many things within this day to give thanks for. Caleb kept his eyes open when we talked to him, and he was much more alert. He showed emotion when we prayed, which he hadn't recently shown. He agreed to get out of his wheelchair and walk from outside to inside his room. And I was especially thankful for Caleb's own heart full of trump cards that his memory loss hadn't touched.

We continued to pray that his short-term amnesia would begin to clear, and we believed every day was one day closer. We thanked God for giving us signs along the way, according to HIStory.

TBI MANIPULATION

There had been many ways used to manipulate Caleb to do a task he refused to do, and there were times when he had manipulated others as well. I received a message from Caleb's house mom saying he'd participated in the day's therapies but had been quite annoyed while doing so. The agitation seemed to stem from his new medicine regime and the fear that comes with a heightened awareness of not knowing exactly where you are every day, versus where you are accustomed to being—for example, in college every day. Though Caleb had been at Touchstone for a month and could mostly remember where he was, he still didn't remember events from the day before. Leaving in the evenings became a little easier, because Caleb trusted we'd come back the next day, even if he didn't remember that we had been there for all of his yesterdays.

I arrived at Touchstone this evening armed with my bag of manipulative tools, as usual. The mint chocolate chip ice cream was a sure bet, and it worked again to persuade Caleb to go outside. It was a treat for both of us to be sitting in the warm sun and eating ice cream with one another absent the agitation from earlier in the day. He called to visit with his dad after the last spoonful, and Kurt heard a strength in Caleb's voice that he hadn't heard only two days prior. Caleb's stride also showed increased vigor as I helped him from his wheelchair, complimenting him on how well he was walking. Removing his hand tentatively from its grip on my arm, Caleb determinedly walked independently of my help for the first time.

As an evening filled with many blessings drew to an end, Caleb correctly remembered his age being twenty-one, and recalled reading the book series *The Hunger Games* right before Christmas. His manipulation surfaced when he suggested that we compete in a *Hunger Games* "knowledge bowl" contest to see who could have his back scratched the longest. I was at a distinct disadvantage, having not read the books. I feel certain Caleb won the competition, but no doubt about it, his brain was figuring out ways for him to also win during the days ahead.

TRASH FISH

Caleb had an army of friends supporting him, both pre-injury and post-injury. On a mid-April Saturday four committed ones came to Windsor House, bearing his favorite lunch from Chipotle and a willingness to spend the day with him. As they gathered around the conference room table, Caleb and Kurt left the room and then reappeared minutes later, smiling … this time without his wheelchair. He wanted to show off.

Interacting more than we had seen him do in a very long time, Kurt and I left this generation alone to enjoy their lunch, knowing they'd watch over Caleb and then meet us outside. I watched in awe as a smiling Caleb slowly walked out the front door toward the basketball court, supported by a friend on each side and two others on close standby if needed. With encouragement from his friends, Caleb grasped the basketball, steadied himself in front of a ten-foot goal, slowly lifted the ball to his chest, and with much determination and effort made his shot count! It was Cabe's first post-injury attempt since his pre-injury intramural days at A&M, and it required much more from him, mentally and physically, than any three-pointer made during a March madness game.

The acre pond on the grounds of Touchstone sits fifty yards away from the outdoor court, and at this time of year it was covered almost completely with lily pads. We all slowly relocated to its grassy bank at the water's edge where we hoped for a fish as Kurt cast into the waters. Reclining on a blanket spread on the ground, Caleb willingly got up only moments later to reel in the fish tugging at the end of Kurt's line. It wasn't an easy reel for Cabe through the thick aquatic plant life, and it turned out the catch wasn't a fish tugging at the end of his line, but rather a swollen plastic grocery bag!

Even more incredible was Caleb's effort to get to a standing position again only minutes later when Kurt yelled, "Fish on, Caleb!" after having already been fooled once. He reeled in a really nice largemouth bass (which wouldn't shame either of them), and it was team fishing at its best. The group enjoyed the blessings that come with being outdoors and looking at all life has to offer, trash included. Not only did we enjoy the coolness of the breeze, but we watched it move the lily pads gently over the water's surface while turtles popped their little heads out from underneath.

Caleb didn't want these moments to end, and he tirelessly asked his friends not to leave but to stay longer. They obliged and supported Caleb on their walk back to Windsor House to spend more time in his room. Watching Caleb labor to make the hundred-yards toward Kurt and me, I once again received a clear picture of what a Christian brother looks like. He is one who walks with you in support, to keep you from falling.

All of us prayed for Caleb, and then we reluctantly told his guests they needed to get back on the road. As he lay in bed, his friends made their way toward the bedroom door, only to hear Caleb call Kyle back for one last good-bye and hug—or so I thought. Instead he took Kyle's hand and told him, "Stay strong in the Lord, Brother." Even from our healing beds we can encourage one another, and here was Caleb, through his words and God's work in him, being the encourager. Kalina testified of God's work, telling Caleb about the last time they had come to see him, and about their commitment to pray for him to walk; and he had. We were all encouraged.

Friends as well as family continued to visit, and on this particular Sunday, family visitors brought Jazzy, our dog. Everyone hoped when Jazz's mega pounds of love and affection greeted Caleb for the first time, he would unequivocally declare that there was *no way* this was a dream. Our hopes were followed by disappointment when Caleb's delight in seeing Jazz didn't mimic the Hollywood ending you see in movies. In fact, the sunshine from the day before was hidden, and raindrops began to fall. We reloaded Jazz into the car and returned her to her temporary home, and Caleb returned to his.

Recalling the morning's worship services at April Sound Church, the sermon had been on just that: our temporary home. The prayer over Kurt and me by an elder of the church during the service was comforting, and afterward he excitedly escorted us to meet both pastors. We stood absolutely dumbfounded and *amazed* as we listened to them both tell us they had each suffered a severe brain injury from accidents years before—and had recovered.

It seemed God had once again provided for us in a special way while we were in our temporary home. In spite of this God-given provision, however, I still longed, deep down in my heart, to be in *my* familiar home. And I wanted to take Caleb there with me.

45

LIVING THE DREAM

Caleb continued to walk, independent of his wheelchair, and his body overall was gaining strength. Yet he still talked about the dream. Lying outside on his back during our afternoon visit, he appeared to be pondering something. When asked what his thoughts were, he retorted, "This dream!"

Dr. Cassidy helped us realize that Caleb had no idea what post-traumatic amnesia entailed, so the best Caleb could relate to what he was feeling was a dream state. Having this knowledge, however, didn't make it any easier to watch Caleb lie there and cry, "This has been so long, and I just keep having this same dream." When I asked how long he'd been having this dream, he answered, "Two weeks!" I chose not to tell Caleb how long it had actually been.

Once again, words of conviction from many people—like Suzy, who hadn't seen Caleb in quite a while—gave us a better perspective on the progress he was making. We continued to miss the sum of all the small, positive steps from day to day, even as she testified of her amazement at how much better Caleb was doing.

A woman's words, posted from Japan, saying that she was praying for Caleb, encouraged him after he had expressed to us only hours earlier, "No one even knows what's going on with me." We continued to remind him that today was not a dream, and where we were in this journey was God's plan and for His glory. As we reminded him, it served as another reminder to us also.

The only problem was his amnesia wouldn't let him hold on to any of that truth the next day, and we traveled down the familiar "dream" path all over again. He did seem, however, to have made a conscious choice not to speak to anyone throughout the day, which was reported to us when we got to Touchstone. I'm not sure of any earlier connection, but he opened up to us while having dessert, telling us that he had fallen asleep somewhere and couldn't wake up. He acknowledged his fear of not knowing where he is—when he finally does wake up. We relied upon Dr. Cassidy's knowledge concerning biological healing, assuring Caleb that we didn't solely have our hopes in him. We continued to ask God to awaken Caleb to the truth and to help us see the larger picture around us as we waited.

Our home church continued to pray for Caleb daily, and one day each week was specifically designated for his caregivers and doctors. It was rewarding to hear Shaquetta testify of answered prayers for her family and the movement of God in their lives. We clung to the familiar words of a song that says, "I will trust you while I'm waiting."

While we tried to patiently wait, tents were being erected on the grounds of Touchstone for the annual Family Day.

46

FAMILY DAY

Caleb could be found in front of the television at ten a.m. most summer mornings of his preteen years. He was geared up for Bob and *The Price Is Right,* and he knew every game played, Plinko being his favorite. When we learned part of the activities planned for Family Day included game show themes, the Jentsches felt sure they'd be the winners of their first Family Feud match when they sat down at the table side by side. We did well through the first two questions, and then Caleb became disturbed by the band's music playing close by. Kurt ended up relocating Cabe to a quieter place, while Sarah Kate carried our family to victory by herself.

Family Day was not only an annual event for current Touchstone residents, but also for residents who had been released to their homes throughout the years. We couldn't help but look forward to a day when we would travel back as former residents too. Yet for now, we still waited for that day, knowing God held the roadmap and would reveal this part of His plan when He was ready. We were challenged once again to savor the company of the One who was seeing us through this time while we waited.

As the tents came down late in the afternoon, Caleb seemed to be more aware of his circumstances and more downtrodden than usual. Asked if he hurt anywhere, he replied, "My heart." When our child's heart hurts, we hurt, and because most of us have experienced hurt personally, we can pray with compassion.

A doctor on staff also spoke with Caleb during the Family Day seclusion and noted that his memory seemed to be improving slowly, but it was jagged when compared to a consistent, lucid line they were hoping for. Very few occasions supported the hope that Caleb's short-term memory may be holding, but none was more perfectly displayed than when he greeted us the next evening. His smile was accompanied by, "Did you bring me some pie?" I had, and I was happy to take him outside to enjoy the gift of pie.

Caleb had willingly participated in all the morning's scheduled therapies, and this evening he chose to play a board game after enjoying his gift. The familiar game *Sorry* was one we often played on family game nights at home. As I viewed the places of safety located across the colorful board, I thought about the game much differently than I had in times past. There was "Home," and then there was an actual safety zone—two places to be for protection. I was actually headed to one such place tomorrow after being away for two and half months, while Kurt stayed in Conroe to be with Caleb.

Sarah Kate and I were anxious to see friends and be in our church home, and my anxiety was building as I thought about walking into *our own home* for the first time in a *long* time. Fifteen miles outside of Victoria, God provided the "wink" I needed through my encouraging friend Suzanne, who called to pray for me over the phone. No sooner had she said amen, my tires were touching the pavement of business 59-S. As I looked at the Victoria exit sign suspended above the road and then directly ahead, I looked forward to the day when we would bring Caleb home waving a victory flag.

Missing was the orange-and-black detour sign that had stood weighted by sandbags. Our neighborhood hadn't been accessible via our normal street entrance because of the road construction over the past twelve months. Renovation had ultimately reached our end of the major thoroughfare—the last of three phases taking place over the past four months—and I knew this was a timely correlation to Caleb's path. Though not complete, significant progress had been made over time. God steadied Philippians 1:6 (NIV) in my mind: "being confident of this, that he who began a good work in you will carry it on to completion until the day of Christ Jesus."

It was comforting to talk to Kurt during the evening and know that he was filling in well for me—and was probably doing better in the place where I had always been. Caleb smiled seeing Kurt walk up carrying a Sonic Blast, and I chose to believe his smile was directed more toward his dad than seeing the added blessing of a Blast. "If you, then, though you are evil, know how to give good gifts to your children, how much more will your Father in heaven give good gifts to those who ask him!" (Matthew 7:11 NIV).

Today's words from Kurt and our heavenly Father were consoling as I finally laid my head down at home to sleep. Not only had Caleb smiled at Kurt, he had smiled upon hearing the voice of

Sheena, his house mother, as she entered the room behind where he was seated. After participating in the day's speech therapy but refusing occupational therapy, Caleb had requested to speak with Sheena—personally. Interacting with his one-on-one caregiver throughout the morning, he wanted to help deliver lunch to a resident in a different home. As excited as we were to hear about his desire to participate, it wasn't so much about his asking to deliver lunch. It was about Caleb *remembering* who Sheena was by name and by voice—and *remembering* that she had the authority to permit him to go!

Kurt said smiles were over-the-top contagious amongst the staff— and even more so when a trio of his closest female friends arrived from College Station. Caleb's smiles were now accompanied by, "I am so happy to see you!" It was a divine blessing for Kurt to have this heartwarming experience after having been apart from Caleb for work during the week. With his love tank filled to the brim, Sarah Kate and I were wrapping up a lovely stay in Victoria, experiencing the same.

While I was preparing to leave Sunday afternoon, I had no idea Kurt was loading Caleb into his car to taxi him around the twenty-five acres of Touchstone property. It was deemed Caleb's first pleasure ride, since all previous transports were for medical purposes between facilities, or by wheelchair while he was at one. It had been an *exceptionally* good weekend for all, especially for memory's sake!

The morning before I left my house, which I hadn't seen in seventy-five days, I sat with my coffee by the Christmas tree. It was still standing, though friends had offered to take it down. We were determined to have Christmas again when Caleb returned home, because he would *never* remember the Christmas of 2011. SK and I loaded up suitcases packed with spring clothes to replace the winter garments I had put away, and we slowly backed out of the driveway to head to Conroe.

Noticeably, the seasons had also cycled through a change during our absence. The poinsettia was now dead on the front porch, and the bottle brush stood blooming nearby. Solomon's words from Ecclesiastes 3 resonated with me: there is a time for everything, and everything on earth has its special season. When leaving my home on January 1, 2012, I'd had no clue I would only return for a short visit on April 26. I didn't need to know, because God knew already.

47

THE PERFECT NUMBER

Kurt and Caleb had spent most of the past Saturday afternoon working on holding Cabe's short-term memory amidst his dream state. Resting under Touchstone's shaded, covered parkway between numerous walkabouts around the grounds, Caleb did his best to recall moments just discussed between him and his dad. Physically fatigued and mentally tired of trying, Kurt and Cabe headed to Windsor House to grab some supper, and Caleb was ready for a shower and bed.

As another summer's day came to a close, Kurt asked Caleb to concentrate on holding a specific number for Kurt's return after church the next morning. The number chosen was three, as it relates to the Trinity found only in God's Word. It is an emotional connection between a father and his son, and one they hoped God would honor them for remembering. They prayed with each other at Caleb's bedside, including a reminder to hope for what tomorrow might bring. Hugs given, Caleb crawled into bed and said good night to his dad.

The church setting at April Sound was a little different for Kurt this morning—absent his girls and feeling the anxiousness of seeing Caleb. He didn't really remember the sermon, because his thoughts of remembering lay eight miles away. The sunny day couldn't have been a more perfect stage as Kurt drove into Touchstone, parked his car in front of Windsor House, and buzzed the doorbell to be let inside.

Cabe was up and dressed, had eaten a midmorning breakfast, and was sitting in the living room chatting with his caregivers, Stephanie and Shamequa. He was smiling more these days, and we were thankful for this added blessing. He saw Kurt and said, "Hi, Dad!" Heart pounding, Kurt greeted Caleb in like kind and without delay sat down beside him. Looking intently into Caleb's eyes, Kurt slowly asked for the number he hoped Caleb still held from the night before.

After a blank stare and what seemed like an eternal pause, the mental search softened Caleb's eyes, and a smile grew from ear to ear. Assuredly and almost laughingly, Caleb responded, "Three … the Father, Son, and Holy Spirit!"

It was a praise-the-Lord-from-the-hilltop moment as Kurt joyfully acknowledged the final line of the Doxology: "Praise Father, Son, and Holy Ghost!" Cabe's smile said it all, and Kurt thanked the Father for the trust and confidence in what he was sure they had both hoped for yesterday, and the certainty that He would bring it about today.

This day would mark the beginning of Caleb clearing post-traumatic amnesia— the day the needle would begin to point north in his recovery!

MAY DAY = GOOD DAY

Entering the date "May 1, 2012" was the first step in setting up the Wii game console that we had purchased for Caleb and other residents to play in between structured therapies at Windsor House. Sarah Kate began the task of entering the day's date and year, but the month and day were displayed in each other's places: 1/05/2012. These are two very distinct days, and they proved to be so in Caleb's recovery as well.

Her first entry reflected the exact date when Caleb had been injured and we'd prayed for his life. The second was a day of thanksgiving: that Caleb could remember a few things from the past week and could tell us the correct year. Sarah Kate had put the "1" in the wrong position, and the lesson was clear. God is to be our number One, and always in the first position. He spoke those words to all of us in His command: "You shall have no other gods before me" (Exodus 20:3 NIV).

After spending the afternoon with Cabe, we made a quick trip to College Station to join the BSM students in prayer at their last official prayer gathering for the semester. Their first one had been specifically for Caleb, so it brought us great joy to be a part of their last to share the many answered prayers.

Caleb still grew anxious when our time came to leave, needing reassurance again that we'd return, because "this dream" he spoke about still persisted. Our hope for better days ahead was answered as we read Sheena's earlier e-mail reporting on Caleb's day: "Today was wonderful. He was talking with his one-on-one, and he is oriented to month, day, and year. He wrote a list stating his birthday, the names of his family, days of the week, and months of the year. He also did some simple math problems. He did great in physical therapy and will start programming in the cognitive program. What a joy I feel today!" Not only were we all encouraged in College Station, but we thanked God for those who had ceaselessly worked and prayed to bring Caleb to where he was today.

The next afternoon we quickly tracked Caleb down in his room to personally ask him to tell us what year it was. He responded with 2012! I wanted to blow a party horn and scream "Happy New Year!" It was a huge celebration that Caleb could now consistently recall the correct year (he always had a 2012 calendar hanging in his room at Touchstone), even though he still couldn't remember the correct date. As I prepared May's calendar to hang by his doorway, Kelley spoke our hopes when she shared, "I pray we will not need a June one here."

Our prayer requests went out overnight, asking for Caleb's line of improvement to now move more vertically than horizontally. We witnessed an answer to those prayers the following afternoon when Caleb sang an unsolicited solo in group therapy, only to have Myisha and other caregivers attest that he had been singing all day long. His songs of choice? "His Eye Is on the Sparrow," "How Great Is Our God," and "Come Thou Fount."

Not only was Caleb singing with his fellow residents, but our hearts too were singing, "How great is our God!"

...AND THE GLORY FOREVER

We worked to build relationships while at Touchstone, and some were easier to establish than others. This in itself was a movement of God, because not only did I not want to be at this place when we arrived in March, I didn't want to like the people who were there to help.

We had grown to love the caregivers personally, and knew many of the residents and their families by name. More opportunities for our growth seemed to come with each new day, and today's Cinco de Mayo celebration found us interacting with Windsor residents and caregivers, who were already enjoying the afternoon piñata activities when we arrived. (By the way, it was reported that Caleb had made some really good therapeutic swings at busting the piñata—much to everyone's enjoyment!)

The evening's outdoor activities moved onto the basketball court, and we quickly competed with another resident and his caregiver in a modified game of Around the World and Horse. Kurt's shoot-around with Don enticed a few other residents and caregivers to join in to attempt the rusty goal's ten-foot height, and new relationships began to intertwine. How refreshing it was to hear other residents and caregivers cheering for and applauding one another!

The encouragement didn't even begin to calm down at the Windsor House when Caleb greeted his caregiver at the front door. He looked at Teresa, smiled really big, and said, "Can I give you a hug?" She grinned, grabbed her boy as if he'd made her day, and hugged him—to our delight. *Asking* her for help to recall her name, we then worked together with Caleb to gather a bowl, spoon, cereal and milk from the kitchen for a snack, and a deck of cards for indoor activities.

Don was also in tow behind Kurt for a snack, and they quickly picked up their conversation from where they'd left off outside. Don, a resident who had been relocated to Windsor from the upper East Coast, said he'd heard that Caleb was a world traveler. We asked Caleb to explain to Don why he'd gone to Japan and Paris in his world travels. Cabe's response over his bowl of cereal was simple, direct, and convicting: "To share Jesus. Do you know him?"

Don didn't hesitate to say yes, and minutes later, after some searching, he recited the Lord's Prayer—with a few gaps. When he got to the end, he said, "For thine is the kingdom, and the power, and—" We gladly filled in the blank, sensing what we too were experiencing: "and the glory forever."

I played cards with Caleb, and Kurt played dominoes with Don. In the midst of their game and conversation, Don explained to Kurt why he couldn't remember the end of the prayer. He hadn't prayed it in a long time. Kurt encouraged him to pray it daily so as not to forget, and he personally prayed with Don before we left. He also reminded Don of his commitment to help put together a new basketball goal tomorrow.

Little did Kurt know at the time; he would need Don's commitment to plan B as well.

50

MISSING PIECES

Plan A was to put up a new backboard and rim we'd purchased on Saturday morning. The only problem was, it didn't quite match the outdated pole cemented in the ground—and that was only discovered after Chris helped Kurt loosen the rusty nuts from the original backboard and goal.

Chris was also a resident of Windsor House and one of the first residents we'd met upon moving Caleb to Touchstone in March. He was in his mid-thirties, heavily tattooed, and had a completely shaved head. He had suffered a brain injury in an automobile accident twelve months earlier, and honestly, his appearance and loud voice scared me when we were first introduced. Chris was also one of the saucer-eyed residents who tried to physically intervene when Caleb chased his one-to-one caregiver down the hallway. Chris had developed a healthy respect for Caleb on that day, and we grew to love Chris for who he was, not for what he appeared to be through our judgmental eyes.

Pure and simple, the basketball goal would need to be replaced by a completely different one. Lunchtime offered the guys a timely redirection, so we all stopped to eat and discuss plan B. Chris and Kurt determined that a portable goal sitting on the opposite end of the slab would be the collaborative fix and would allow residents to have two goals to shoot at. This wasn't too much of a setback in the very hot and humid Conroe weather (insert sarcasm), right? So to allow *all* temperatures a chance to cool down, I went and purchased a portable unit while the men rested. The assembly time was reset to begin that evening.

The boys now refreshed and raring to go, the completion wouldn't occur because of yet another setback. With the large box opened and parts strewn everywhere, we seemed to be missing an important bag of nuts, bolts, and accessories to put it all together. Don made a timely suggestion to Kurt to just "jimmy it" with the old parts to make it work.

I immediately thought about how many times I'd made that same request of God on this journey after Caleb's injury. I didn't care if we had the correct pieces or not; I just wanted it to work without the wait! For all intents and purposes, it appeared the wait for the pieces, yet again, would be longer than we anticipated.

Kurt made a prayerful trip back to the store this time and kindly asked a manager to open another box to acquire the parts missing from our original purchase. After opening two different boxes of like units together, they discovered that both lacked this very important bag of necessities. Unbelievable! Kurt was more than frustrated, and we were both in need of being refreshed in the fellowship at April Sound.

We took communion with the body of believers at the church on Sunday morning and later shared in the remembrance again as Pastor Robert traveled to Touchstone to serve us, along with Caleb, Don, and Chris. It blessed our hearts to see Chris kneel slowly to receive the gift representing Christ. The community of Conroe had reached out to Touchstone—and to us in a time of need—and it was a special time for all of us to remember what truly matters most.

Tired, we again rested during the heat of the afternoon. Kurt then made the last run to the local hardware store to round-up the pieces needed to complete the work started the evening before. In the meantime, we celebrated Caleb's memory of the incomplete basketball goal and why it hadn't been assembled on two different occasions. Along with celebrating his memory, we gave thanks that he was walking unassisted with a spotter and could remove his shoes and get dressed with some help.

Kurt was able to put the goal together before dark with the steadfast help of his welcomed assistants. Chris was Kurt's right-hand man, and Don was his left. Caleb appeared to be content just watching. Unlike Chris, Don had suffered two traumatic brain injuries three years apart in unrelated accidents during his adolescent years. He had been in and out of several recovery units from the upper East Coast to Texas, finding his current home at Touchstone. It was a joy for Kurt to see his willing helpers give him instructions on how best to manage the assembly, maneuver wrenches, and lift the weight of the goal the best they could.

With the production almost complete and many beads of perspiration lost, I suddenly heard Kurt holler out, "They're here!" He was, of course, referring to the bag of missing pieces. It was packed purposefully in a box within a concealed compartment inside the larger box, well hidden from sight. We couldn't speculate on why they'd been efficiently placed where they were or why we'd been made to trudge through a hot weekend with so much effort to do something that looked to be so good. We were reminded of the scripture from Luke 15 where Jesus told the parable of the lost sheep. He said, "What appears to have been lost, now is found." In the story, the owner calls his neighbors together when the lost sheep is found and says, "…Rejoice with me; I have found my lost sheep" (Luke 15:6 NIV).

Leaving the grounds of Touchstone as the sun was setting, Bill was still outside, swishing close-range baskets with a steadying hand from his caregiver. His earlier shots hadn't been successful, because the old goal's height was fixed. Bill just didn't have the strength yet to reach the rim. The new goal was adjustable to different heights, and we now understood why our "plan A" wouldn't have met every resident's needs.

Kurt related it to us, saying, "It's just like God. He meets us where we are. He is never unreachable." The Word of God says it even better in Romans 5:6–8 (NIV): "You see, at just the right time, when we were still powerless, Christ died for the ungodly. Very rarely will anyone die for a righteous man, though for a good man someone might possibly dare to die. But God demonstrates his own love for us in this: While we were still sinners, Christ died for us."

That's what we remember as we eat the bread and take the wine. There are no missing pieces with Him.

51

JUST ANOTHER MONDAY? NOPE.

I hated that Kurt had to leave a day early after working so hard to put the basketball goal up over the weekend. I really wanted him to have a day of rest before going back to work in Victoria. Nonetheless, it allowed Sarah Kate and me to be busy in the Conroe house doing Monday chores of dusting and ironing.

The fight to keep my mind on the right path was difficult, and I appreciated the message I heard through SK's DVD about Abraham and the faithful life he'd lived. Then I heard the story of Joseph and his brothers and how unfair it seemed that Joseph was going through such injustice. So the battle raged between what I was hearing on the DVD and what I was thinking in my head.

I was thinking about a lost semester at A&M, the upcoming plans Caleb had made for summer that wouldn't take place, and what I had been doing the year before. I had to make a choice either to take my thoughts captive and make them obedient to Christ as found in Galatians 5:8 or to serve myself at my own pity party. I could think on the things required in Philippians 4:8, or tell myself that I deserve to think what I want.

Thankfully, that day I chose to thank God for Kurt's safe trip home, for a day spent with Sarah Kate, for friends who came to see Caleb and love on SK, for being greeted at the door with a smile by residents and caregivers, for the progress Caleb was making, for the opportunity to be close to Caleb so I could see him daily, and for the followers and prayers on the CaringBridge site who encouraged us so. There was too much to be thankful for to let the circumstances weigh me down. Little did I know, I'd also want to throw a thankfulness party by the day's end!

Supper concluded, we retreated outside where Caleb requested to call Kurt to visit about their workdays. With Dad's good-bye, Caleb turned to me for some memory Q & A time together and he tried his hardest to answer my questions correctly. His brain was beginning to hold on to not only what he was personally experiencing, but also accepting memory of the experiences that he had been told he would've never remembered on his own. When finally getting around to asking him a big question— where he was, and why—he responded, "Touchstone, because I had a skiing accident."

My question list and I were exhausted, so Caleb called Kyle to extend the inquisition. Kyle asked him similar questions, and then asked *the* question I had wearily thought about but avoided asking verbally: "Does this feel like a dream?" Caleb replied, "No." Hallelujah, and praise the Lord! I had feared asking *the* question, but it was now inked on *my list of queries* to ask when quizzing Caleb again.

The next day the questions continued at Caleb's invitation after his visiting friends arrived. The best of all came from Caleb himself when they were departing: "Can y'all come back tomorrow?" He'd enjoyed their visit so much he wrote down the names of everyone present so he wouldn't forget. Then he shared them with Kurt over the phone as he cheerfully recalled what a good day it had been.

We all looked forward to another good one after Dr. Cassidy saw Caleb on Friday morning and then met with us for his bimonthly report. I anxiously awaited his glowing review filled with notes about the progress that I felt sure was obvious to anyone. Yet as the day arrived, I read the e-mail saying Doctor John was sick and wouldn't be present. Greatly disappointed, I remembered that this was no surprise to God, only to me.

The team meeting took place with Caleb's therapists, nurse, and house mom, and all reports were grand—especially since Caleb appeared to be clearing post-traumatic amnesia, and his agitation was almost nonexistent.

They entertained our prepared question about taking Caleb away from the facility on a Saturday day pass to the lake house, and my hopes were high. We aimed to leverage our safe care of Caleb, since we were already taking him to a scheduled off-site appointment during the week to have his feeding tube removed— the one he hadn't used since February. And as for my future *hopes* of being back *home* anytime soon in Victoria—well, they weren't even given any consideration, as discussions *now* turned toward beginning more intensive therapies over the next few months. I responded to this news by requesting friends pray both for my patience and for Kurt's endurance in traveling back and forth to work four hundred miles each week.

I likened this whole meeting to the music we hear and how we hear it. When I read the e-mail stating that Dr. Cassidy couldn't be present, I was not singing out joyful words, but just hearing the background music still calmed me. When I heard the words that Caleb was clearing PTA, I was most definitely belting out a happy tune for all to hear! And then, when the revelation came that our stay would be extended for a few more months, it was as if someone had scratched the needle across the top of my spinning vinyl album—as only someone close to my age can relate to. I was disheartened until a softer, gentler song soothed me as outside passes for Caleb were being considered. I found a YouTube video of the Brooklyn Tabernacle Choir singing "My Life Is in Your Hands" and let the song wash over me after leaving the meeting.

The next day I heard a new song, which had been sent to me in January, but I hadn't recalled it until this evening while sitting in Touchstone's conference room. I watched five college-aged young adults do the WOP, play *Fishbowl*, and sing a wide genre of songs. The new song was the one Liz reminded Caleb that he had introduced them to the previous fall while in Wimberley, Texas. They sang the chorus in unison: "Never once did we ever walk alone. Never once did you leave us on our own. You are faithful, God, you are faithful."

As my tears dropped, Caleb was singing, and there's no way you can buy or wrap a gift containing that much value. I could only respond, "Thank You." Only the night before I had grieved at the thought of being here, and tonight I wondered why in the world I would want to be anywhere, but here. I watched as Caleb and Alex embraced to say good-bye, and then I heard Caleb charge him to spread the name of Jesus and make Him famous.

I hadn't received a report on Caleb's therapies for the day, but I knew mine had been phenomenal. If his had been even half of what mine had been over the past two hours, they were more than enough. The experiences of God are therapeutic: "Buy from me medicine to put on your eyes so you can truly see" (Revelation 3:18 NCV).

TRANSITIONING

With his post-traumatic amnesia clearing, we were continuing to see evidences of improvement in many areas of Caleb's healing. His physical stamina and abilities showed marked gains, though he was still deficient in many ways.

Caleb and Kurt were outside hitting tennis balls on the versatile concrete slab when Sarah Kate and I arrived. We watched him gently return balls at the pace Kurt was feeding them to him, only to see him lace them past Kurt after requesting Caleb add some topspin. He had the ability to extend his arm from his side but wouldn't mobilize his feet and body to move beyond his reach. His balance while standing was adequate, but wobbly and unsure when he attempted to turn. That tended to unnerve me. I feared a fall and a setback. Therapies addressed his basic needs, but I wanted him protected under all circumstances.

The weight gain from eating balanced meals and many desserts (our bad) also allowed Caleb to put back on much more weight than the thirty pounds he'd lost during the first six weeks, and more than likely contributed to his instability. His hair was also growing out and beginning to cover his eight-inch semicircular scar. Mentally, we had celebrated many successes, but Caleb still could not remember who had visited the day before unless given clues to help him. Though he couldn't remember the specifics of a prior visitor, he could now remember the joy of the experience. That was what drove his desire to remember more. The most marked deficit was energy. Every action, whether getting dressed or mentally answering questions, was a drain on Caleb's energy meter.

While we tried to focus on his improvements versus his deficiencies, I hate to confess that I feared losing the support of many who had been faithful to encourage us through prayer, visits, and hosts of other actions. It was a struggle within, because I didn't want Caleb to lose such grandiose support, yet I felt selfish when I continued to ask to draw from others.

This was when we also realized that it was as much a time to give as to receive, and our relationships with others at Touchstone became much more personal. Caleb's interactions became more fluid with his caregivers and other residents, calling them by name and loving them in the process of spending a lot of time together. This became even more evident as he began to be able to leave the facility on day passes.

53

UP AND AWAY

On May 12, 2012, Caleb officially took a leave of absence from the care facility and was solely in our care. He entered the CaringBridge post from the lake house and started by saying, "Howdy, everyone. This is Caleb Jentsch. Today was a very good day! I was walking around my whole house today (Windsor House) and saw my dad there to pick me up. He then drove me to where they were staying, and I went in the front door to see my mom!"

It wasn't what he said that was so spectacular. It was that he was able to say it. He confirmed in the update that his love for the Lord had stayed the same and that he continued to sing when he could. He thanked those who were praying for him and asked they keep it up so his brain would continue to heal and he could move out of Touchstone. He attested to the fact that it was God's timing and he needed to be patient. *Me too*, I thought after reading his entry.

What a joyful time it was to spend together. Caleb walked barefoot in the grass and sat by the peaceful lake. In the midst of being away from the daily schedule at Touchstone, Caleb asked if therapies were taking place, because he didn't want to miss any. We reminded him it was Saturday, and no therapies occurred on weekends. But Monday was coming. When quizzed to remember what Monday held in store, he was quick to reply that his feeding tube was coming out. It was these small remembrances that reminded us the needle was still pointing in the desired direction.

Caleb did so well on his day pass that another was allowed the following day—Mother's Day. I was really looking forward to going to worship with one another, but Caleb ended up being too tired, and stayed behind with Kurt at the house. It was a gift from April Sound Church to hear a message on heaven and to know God has a place already prepared for us.

Singing the lyrics "strength will rise when we wait upon the Lord" as a body was like another sermon to my soul. This song brought back the remembrance of Caleb singing it with the youth praise band at church. On that Sunday morning years before, there had been an excitement I will never forget, and others had spoken of it as well. It was just good to hear the lyrics again today proclaiming that the everlasting Lord doesn't faint or grow weary defending the weak, and that He comforts those in need while lifting us all up on wings like eagles.

The time of worship, Caleb being with us, the beautiful day, and much more made this Mother's Day a day to remember.

NO MORE CORD

Though it hadn't been used for feeding or medication since February, Caleb's PEG tube was only now being removed three months later. We had requested many times for it to be gone since it wasn't being used, but were wisely informed—even though it had caused Caleb no discomfort—it was best to stay in for the "what ifs" we were not anticipating. To have to insert another tube at some point would be more unnecessary pain for Caleb to endure—and now remember. We had already *been there and remembered that* with Caleb's help.

I couldn't convince the team there would be no future need for it, and I finally decided it was best to try to let it go. I now feared for Cabe's pain when having it removed. It seemed my fears were unfounded, and the pain of removing it was nonexistent after Caleb and Kurt exited the examining room following a two-minute procedure. We were thankful and prayed for the other residents who had had their tubes for such a long time because they were not able to swallow correctly.

The removal of the tube gave us opportunity to share with Caleb the scares—and the laughter—it had provided us on rare occasions.

In earlier days we had feared that Caleb would pull his tube out when he was agitated—which he had indeed succeeded in doing while under the distracted care of his one-to-one soon after arriving at TIRR. At this low-point he began wearing a Velcro binding around his midsection to prevent him from doing so again.

The laughter came when Caleb expressed that he was pregnant and the tube was the connector between him and his baby. Some pretty crazy stories accompanied his theories, and we went along with most of them. We finally just said *no* to one theory that the baby in his stomach was Jesus. We assured him Jesus was in his heart, but pregnancy had nothing to do with it!

Caleb found comic relief in hearing these personal stories, and after a lunch celebrating his tube removal, we returned him to Touchstone to spend time on the treadmill for physical therapy. At the end of this day, we were very thankful Caleb's body showed one less physical sign of the devices used to sustain his life. Thank you, Lord. Caleb was tubeless.

On the Tuesday following tube removal day, Caleb continued to say how glad he was that his PEG was gone. He hadn't complained lately about it being there, but he was certainly glad it wasn't now, which was really about the only thing he was excited about. He had experienced a great day in therapy and said that he had done something really fun. The only problem was—he couldn't remember what it was, and there were no caregivers at Windsor who could remind him because of their afternoon shift change. Though it frustrated him, it was enough just to know Caleb had enjoyed a day that he could now remember into the evening around the game room table while playing *Apples to Apples* together.

Lori was visiting again, and of course she brought dewberry pie. Not only did she bring pie; she also brought good news of the improvements she was witnessing since her last visit two weeks before. She noted that Caleb's attention span was increasing, which was echoed by his caregiver after playing the game with us. The lively interaction between everyone brought laughter, and Caleb ended up winning, fair and square. His ability to read and comprehend throughout the game was both convincing and encouraging—it was the vision in his right eye, however, that was troubling him and would soon be checked out.

Much of the same laughter followed the next day, only in greater doses. After three hours of physical and mental activity, the evening wound down, and I was pretty much worn out. I'd been Caleb's only spotter while he "bumped" a volleyball around his circle of visiting friends outside. A game of iPad *Family Feud* followed next, only to be continued indoors with *Apples to Apples* and a game called *Fishbowl*. There was one piece of dewberry pie left for a between-game snack, and Caleb whole-heartedly assured everyone that had there been more, he would've shared.

The games served to stimulate Caleb's brain, and I sympathized with a notable caregiver who was excited to be invited into the group, but was greatly handicapped for doing so. Because all these friends attended Texas A&M University and had played these games with each other over the course of the past three years, they had their own lingo. When certain words placed in the fishbowl appeared—such as "Rudder Tower," "Kyle Field," "Joel Bratcher," and "Reed Arena"—you knew you'd been set up by a team of Aggies.

It made me think about how we Christians do this same thing. We use our "church" and "Bible" words. They are spoken most often with meaning and emotions attached, but they're not always understood by everyone we are communicating with. I was reminded once again to speak to and love people where they are, understanding that *my* words are of the least importance. Even though our caregiver was at a distinct disadvantage and I felt bad for him, it was the joy of the experience that was important. Shannon laughed too and delighted in all the shenanigans going on. The laughter carried on until the next day—when Kurt would be back to join the fun.

55

OLD TRICKS

I learned a new word. The word I had to define from the dictionary was *abeyance*. It wouldn't be the first new word I would learn on this journey. The *Jesus Calling* devotion for the day started with, "Come to ME with your plans held in abeyance." I especially liked the second definition I found, which defined it as a condition of undetermined ownership. The devotion continued on to say, "Subordinate your myriad of plans to MY Master Plan."

Just the night before, at the end of four solid hours of interaction with Caleb, we shared that our faith lies not in what we see but in what we don't see. We assured him that we believed God would complete the good work He had started in him many years ago. Although I believed in the outcome and was able to confidently convey it to Caleb, too, I wasn't as good at submitting to the Master's plan myself.

The days were becoming more taxing for Kurt and me. The time we now spent with Caleb was not just sitting and rubbing his feet and encouraging him to talk. Factor in Kurt's being away for several days during the week; we were now missing the emotional support of one another. Both of us were tired at the end of each day, and Sarah Kate was requesting most of our attention when we weren't with Caleb. These were both good "problems" to have, and we wouldn't have wanted either any other way. What a privilege and blessing to end our day with Caleb by having a precious young child only desire to spend the remaining time in our arms. Sometimes being tired is just the gift you need to sit down and enjoy.

Dr. Cassidy would also sit down with our son the following morning, and we were excited for him to see the excellent progress Caleb was making. We prayed their time together would encourage him and that a personal relationship would begin to develop through their conversations. We prayed that Caleb would also love his doctor, since he was now no longer a "dream" to him.

Kurt was back on autopilot from Victoria to spend time with Caleb before SK and I arrived at Touchstone. It was quite the blessing, after the previous months, to walk in and see father and son visiting, just catching up on life's daily happenings. It again revealed a picture of how our heavenly Father intimately desires for us to spend time with Him, sharing the details of our day and listening to Him as well. I believe He even wants to laugh along with us as He stirs up memories in our hearts. The time between this son and his father couldn't have been any richer this evening.

Kurt has been known for the old "there's something on your shirt" trick for many, many years with each of our kids. If they fell for it and looked down towards their chest, he'd flick their nose with his finger. After hugging Caleb good-bye, he pointed at Caleb's shirt and confidently stated, "Cabe, there's something on your shirt."

Caleb smiled and looking directly into Kurt's eyes, pursed his lips, not even daring to look down. Kurt repeated himself, ever so compellingly, and Caleb started laughing. Kurt tried his hardest to stay composed. "No, really, Caleb, there is!" The moment was side-splittingly funny to Caleb, and we all laughed really hard. I don't know for sure what he was thinking, but possibly it was, "There are some things I've fallen for enough times that I will *never* forget." The old trick was some of the best medicine, which he hadn't taken since his accident, and it felt so very, very good.

56

CAPERNAUM

I loved the pattern developing and rejoiced every time Caleb requested to do more, as he'd done when visiting with Dr. Cassidy this week. As games ensued most evenings instead of his desire to go to bed, it was quite evident the participants were different tonight. Instead of attempting to guess "Justin Bieber's closet" when the college group was playing *Fishbowl*, we were now trying to guess "Capernaum."

Our friend and pastor from Victoria had stopped by with his family on their way to Dallas, just as they had come to visit us numerous times in each location we'd called home over the past four months. The Bible mentions Capernaum frequently because of Jesus's presence there. The citizens of this town overlooking the Sea of Galilee were given ample opportunity to hear Jesus speak and to personally experience His awesome redeeming power and love. I'm so thankful we've never had to wonder if Jesus was going to be present at the next location Caleb was transferred to. In each place, the Holy Spirit was already ahead of us, making a way.

Death too was a very real experience we witnessed in both Colorado and Texas. In Denver we watched from across the hall as friends and family struggled for days to say good-bye to the one they loved on life support. At TIRR it was a very sudden "code blue," and loved ones didn't have the opportunity to say good-bye. At Touchstone this past day, Mr. P. had heart complications that left a grieving widow and daughter in disarray. In the midst of each of these families, the God of peace was present, and we prayed He had made a difference.

God's reassurance would also find our own family again as one of Caleb's first caregivers told us about her times of intense prayer with Caleb during some of his most difficult days. Aquila was now seeing such remarkable progress in Caleb and believed that God was doing a good work. She represented Jesus well. We were more than thankful for the caregivers of faith that God had placed around Caleb and the other residents. The words in *Jesus Calling* the next morning were most appropriate: "Jesus is always with us, ready to pick us up when we stumble or fall." No doubt, these caregivers and friends were literally Caleb's arms and feet while he couldn't be.

Through the experiences of the past five months, our territory was expanding, and Caleb's friends and their families were now ours also. The community church family Kurt, SK, and I had joined with in Conroe, would become Caleb's new family as well. His first morning at April Sound Church was high school senior recognition Sunday, and Kurt had been wise to tell Caleb before arriving that sitting through an hour-long service was good therapy.

Caleb participated in the singing, though he only stood for a short while. He sat through the whole service, and whether it was for therapy or for the Luby's Cafeteria meal afterward, he accomplished another step to the north. The weekends when Caleb joined us from rising until bedtime were full days. Packed into them, along with church, were games, homework sheets I prepared, visitors, fishing from the pier (with Dad), and memory work. The TIRR weekends we'd once dreaded due to lack of activity were now replaced by weekends we looked forward to, full of much activity.

Upon returning to Touchstone, Caleb asked if he'd be allowed to do this every weekend. I was so pleased to say, *"Yes*, Caleb. The Lord is good, a refuge in times of trouble!"

57

ANNIVERSARY

Caleb said "I'm sorry" when he learned Kurt and I were spending our anniversary apart for the first time in thirty-one years. As I watched the sunrise that morning, it was a glimpse of what our life had been like during those years. The sun came up slowly over the horizon, and it was beautiful until the dark clouds gradually covered the skyline, and the sun disappeared. Within thirty minutes the clouds were gone, and the sun was shining brightly once again.

Neither Kurt nor I would choose to live those dark-cloud years over again, but they did prepare us for what we would face together with Caleb more than twenty years later. After seven years of marriage we chose a path we had not followed in the beginning years of our marriage and we turned away from each other. We had a choice to make at that time, and we both willfully decided to trust God and not our own feelings. He was faithful then—and He continues to be now—to lead us in the midst of our circumstances if we will only let Him.

Even if Kurt and I couldn't be with each other for our special day, we celebrated anyway. We had too much to celebrate to be sad. Sarah Kate, *being such the girl*, showed me a fancy dress and shiny jewelry she felt sure I should wear to Touchstone, even if Dad wouldn't be there. I'm sure Caleb was more than glad I'd dressed in my normal attire since his friends Hannah and Emily were visiting.

Without any distraction, they helped Caleb reinsert recent memories from the semester before his injury, and it was cool to hear them tell of their own friendship developing as a result of praying together for Caleb. There was no way we could've known then that they would later graduate and serve the Lord side by side as teachers for a year.

This Wednesday hadn't been a normal day of activity at Touchstone, though Caleb was only beginning to remember what he had been doing or who he had seen from day to day. Today was more general than specific. He showed me a picture of a brain on a worksheet and pointed to where he'd drawn a circle. "This is the area of the brain I injured," as Caleb recalled from his brain injury class. Along with short-term memory being stored in the right front temporal lobe, music memory/pitch is also located there, but we never would've known it. While the American Idol finals were being broadcast on television, my own personal artist was serenading me.

Caleb sang "Happy Anniversary," "Never Once," and an Eli Young song he had recently downloaded to his phone. He closed his eyes as he always does when singing, and sang each note and every word without missing a beat. I soaked in the music and thought, "Wow, this must be somewhat how God feels when we sing praises to Him." Humbly speaking, it's not about how we sound, but that we take the time to honor Him.

Caleb had honored me. Upon opening *Jesus Calling* the next morning, I read Zephaniah 3:17: "The LORD Your God is with you ... He will rejoice over you with singing." I realized Caleb was not only singing to me, but God was Himself.

YOUR CHOICE

I would choose this day to listen for God's singing over me, and it needed to be a conscious choice before our team's scheduled morning meeting. We were excited about Dr. Cassidy seeing Caleb after his absence the week before, and we hoped he'd acknowledge the gains Kurt and I believed we were seeing in his healing.

Upon our arrival, we learned from Caleb that he'd had his customary visit with Dr. Cassidy in his room at Windsor House, and then another meeting, unbeknownst to us, with the whole team. He felt unsure and anxious about how both had gone, and we assured him we'd secure the assessment and report back to him.

As he and his caregiver exited the hallway, we entered the conference room and sat at the table surrounded by medical staff and therapists. Statistically speaking, Dr. Cassidy described Caleb as having beaten *all the odds* at this point in his recovery, finally breaking post-traumatic amnesia after four and a half months. When questioned, Dr. Cassidy said that he'd only treated one other patient who had maintained a longer duration. Though he didn't elaborate or specifically say no when we asked, we don't think he really knew if Caleb would have ever cleared the amnesia.

The doctor and therapists were very factual in explaining Caleb's progress, and it seemed they were exercising extreme caution when doing so. As a mother, I wanted to hear more about the gains than the deficiencies, the glass being half full instead of half empty. I wanted to be encouraged. They were not at all trying to discourage me, but they were guarded in how they conveyed what they'd observed.

As for my choosing to still hear the singing, the music was now being drowned out by the words "six months" as the doctor was attempting to explain the brain's healing process. At that precise moment, right outside the building where we were meeting, a train came barreling down the tracks, blaring its horn. And it felt like it was coming straight at me! I *could not* believe they were planning on keeping Caleb for another six months!

Since I wasn't receiving warm fuzzies from the meeting's assessment of Caleb, it gave me great pleasure to hear Kurt tell Dr. Cassidy that we weren't solely relying on him to heal Caleb. We were thankful for each one in attendance and their appointed roles in helping him. Everyone in that room would tell you traumatic brain injuries are accompanied by multiples of the unpredictable, and Kurt and I couldn't have agreed more. Yet we factored in the heart and power of a faithful God. It was a good end to a meeting with all nodding in agreement as Kurt confidently declared, "I can't wait until the day you stand in awe."

Later I began to process aloud with Kurt what I'd heard earlier, after expressing how disappointed I was with the outcome of the meeting. Kurt kindly explained that what I thought I'd heard was not actually what had been said. Dr. Cassidy was in no way suggesting that Caleb remain at Touchstone for another six months. He was only referencing the best timeline in relation to the brain's greatest capacity to heal.

Disappointed in myself, I wished I hadn't let the sounds in my head interfere with the verse I'd heard this morning. After refocusing, I was now sure of the music being sung over me when we reported back to Caleb.

59

HOLY BASS!

Caleb reminded us many times that a three-day weekend was approaching. He wanted to be sure we had secured the required day passes to be with us for all three.

Saturday was a fun, relaxing day spent in the sun, playing games, and watching movies. The only issue a family movie presented was Caleb's inability to follow the storyline for any length of time. The best movies were those he'd already seen years before, which didn't require his short-term memory to hold pace with the next DVD chapter. So we watched and laughed at a funny movie we could all remember together.

Kurt checked Caleb out on Sunday morning and he attended church services and then rested before his friends from Victoria visited. They watched videos posted online, and reminisced about their times with each other in class and at dances. We got a lot of pleasure watching him laugh with friends visiting during weekend passes, and it was especially sweet to hear him sincerely say good-bye and "Thanks for coming to see me."

Kurt spent a lot of time early Sunday morning and all afternoon trying to hook a bass for Caleb to reel to the bank, but absolutely *no* fish were interested in biting. Caleb would participate for a while, tire out, and then go back to the house ten yards away and await his call to come reel. It was quite disheartening for Kurt to enter the house after many hours of intermittent casting to answer "Not yet, Caleb" to the question that everyone else was thinking.

It was during one of these fishing breaks, "the dream" doldrums resurfaced. We knew better this time and addressed the positive side of the conversation when hearing his word choices. In deep thought and with much meekness, Caleb slowly asked Kurt if he could pose a question. "Dad, what can I tell you … if this dream doesn't feel real?" The key descriptor was "feel," and Kurt patiently explained the difference between what we *feel* and what truly *is*. Caleb had been claiming for months, "It is a dream," and we had begrudgingly disputed—to no avail.

Kurt spoke to Caleb about fearing reality and about how God was allowing Caleb to again be pressed in this moment. While they were talking, I was filling time slots with the names of those who had committed to pray for Caleb during a specific hour each day. It became evident that Satan was nudging Caleb to ask the question and had quickly pulled out his "dream card," since this concern hadn't been spoken of in a while. Oh, how painful this conversation must have been for the sneaky snake to see. His plan was falling apart, and Caleb was proclaiming the reality. We told Caleb that God's people were committed to praying bigger, stronger, and more expectantly, and Satan was frantic. Caleb confessed that Satan is a deceiver and wants us to be confused. It was clearly a divine revelation to all three of us at that very moment, and Kurt took it one step further by declaring a victory, *emphatically* telling Caleb, "God is going to give you a fish!"

Heading quickly out the back sliding glass door with rod and reel in hand, I responsively mocked, "Really? Well, then, bring me the coins from its mouth after you do!" I finished warming up dinner and was setting Caleb's in front of him when Sarah Kate sprang to the back door and screamed through the glass, *"Hurry, Caleb, hurry! Dad has a fish for you to reel in!"*

Kurt had stepped outside and slowly walked back and forth along the bank's manicured edge between two neighboring piers, asking God where to cast his first line. Looking for signs on the water, there were none. His feet finally stopped ten yards from the back porch, and God said to him, "Make your first cast straight from here." The weighted plastic lizard settled on the lake's bottom fifteen yards out and was lifted once when Kurt laughingly set the hook against the two-pound largemouth provision for Caleb to reel to the bank.

A perfect Kodak moment captured an experience that was not just *good* fun, but *God* fun! We all were delighted (mostly Kurt and I), because we knew God was helping us understand that we need to simply believe Him for what He tells us! I hope that picture of Caleb holding the fish remains framed in our family for generations to come with the scripture reminding us: "Great is the LORD and most worthy of praise; his greatness no one can fathom. One generation commends your works to another; they tell of your mighty acts" (Psalm 145:3–4 NIV).

While the "catch of the day" made our day complete, there was an added blessing that arrived later in the afternoon. Caleb's visit with cousin KK was chock-full of laughter, and it was hard for him to leave the extended fun to return to Touchstone. Yet in God's goodness, Caleb's words were sweet and prophetic when arriving back to Touchstone: "Home, sweet home," … but not for long.

Caleb rang the bell and walked into Windsor House, greeting all the caregivers with a broad smile. This house had truly become his home away from home. Kurt continued to fish late into the evening, hoping to snag a bonus bass for Sarah Kate. No surprise—it didn't happen. Only one fish had been directed to bite on this day, and we named him the Holy Bass!

THE REALITY OF NOT REMEMBERING

It seemed somewhat strange when Caleb started remembering. He was just beginning to realize what he couldn't remember. His short-term memory was rocking toward the end of May, able to recall visitors, events, and questions posed to him. As he sat with friends on Memorial Day, they were his help to piece together the ski trip in January. Though he was remembering short-term, he would never recall the six months leading up to and including the accident, or the four and a half months spent in amnesia afterward. As time moved forward, we would become aware that this was a blessing we were not yet counting.

To help Caleb create a memory, stories needed to be repeated numerous times. It proved to be very difficult to hear a story he couldn't remember, especially when he was a significant part of it. Along with being told what had happened, Caleb began struggling to control the frustration an injured brain deems as a normal response after it considers the gravity of reality. His spirit was down, and he was in need of encouragement. Our friend Iris reminded Caleb of feelings one might have toward the end of a high school career. With the end in sight, a student might simply like to coast toward the finish line. She encouraged him with words her husband spoke over and over to their own children: "Finish strong!"

Though his spirits were down, everything else was looking up. He was walking to and from all therapies and rarely used his wheelchair. His voice was becoming stronger, and his thinking much clearer. Games of *Monopoly* found him slowly managing banking and real estate transactions with determination and accuracy. Physically and mentally, the needle was pointing more due north, and now it was time to assess his eye and what needed to be done.

The light Dr. Benz was shining into Caleb's right eye revealed something very different from what the nurse's light had revealed four months earlier. Pupil activity had been the goal in January while Caleb had lain unresponsive in TICU. Now we were all very thankful for the new objective as we watched this specialist intently do the same.

Keystone Ski Patrol had originally radioed Flight for Life and said Caleb's right pupil had been "blown" when describing his initial vitals from the scene. Their assessment had been more about his survival than about any concerns for his vision at the time. A month later, TIRR physicians also corroborated the damage during his initial physical exam, assuring us it wouldn't worsen as we again addressed his greater needs at this point in time.

Caleb was now attesting to blurriness while reading, and Dr. Benz scripted onto his chart all he observed, using colored markers to explain why. Concluding that Caleb could wait on a simple

SpillWay

surgery to remove the build-up of floating particles that shouldn't be there, the surgery to correct his vision was postponed for a future time.

We celebrated over a Pazookie dessert following our lunch and were thankful again for another answered prayer. Caleb's humor kept us smiling, and he requested we make an eye appointment every Friday so his workweek could be shortened. Lunch and laughter complete, we went to the mall for exercise and then headed to the house to rest, as most men prefer to do after a mall trip. Caleb was willing to return to Touchstone early for bed, since the weekend ahead looked to be full.

ALL GOOD THINGS...

Caleb had such a wonderful weekend with friends and family; he didn't want the weekend to end. He was beginning to tell us many times over how much he wished he could stay with us full time. I refrained from telling him how many times that I'd had this same thought and wanted to take him away. He took the initiative to do his own physical therapy between visitors at the house, completing reps of mostly slow sit-ups to help try to counter his weight gain, while Sarah and her friend Riley swam in the lake.

Riley and SK had met for the first time at April Sound Church. She is the daughter of Pastor Robert and Amy, and was a God provision to Sarah Kate and to us. She and SK were the same age and had the same interests, and her home was located on the exact same street as our lodging, only ten units along the lake to the right.

This warm afternoon turned their interest again to the water and swimming, despite an occasional break to run into the house for a drink or snack. Climbing back down the dock's few steps leading into the lake, the girls both noticed something small struggling to stay afloat nearby. A baby bird had fallen into the water and was unable to use its tiny soaked wings to rescue itself. It was drowning in a humongous lake, and all hope appeared to be lost.

Amy, responding to their squealing pleas for help, quickly rolled up her pants legs and grabbed the fishing net to scoop the fledgling to higher ground. Gently laying it out on the grass, she gave the baby bird a chance at life. The young girls watched each small twitch closely, hoping for life to win.

With hesitation, I asked Sarah and Riley if they wanted to pray for it. My reluctance came from not wanting the girls to be disappointed in God if the bird died. Sarah Kate prayed for the bird—and for Caleb at the same time—and then Amy announced their need to leave for Houston. We said good-bye, and Sarah Kate went inside.

I dwelled on my hesitation to pray. I was trying to protect God. He has been teaching me for years that He is God and that He hasn't hired me as His defense lawyer. Sarah Kate anxiously paced back and forth from the house numerous times to check on the lifeless bird struggling outside. At the end of that day, my CaringBridge entry reported the bird was no longer with us. Two hours after its rescue, to our great joy, the youngster flew away. We stood thankful in our state of awe. My heart knew there would be a similar time in our future when Caleb would also spread his wings and no longer be with us; he too would fly into the north wind.

As we returned Caleb to Touchstone, I filled in the blank differently from the way I normally would have. I would have usually chosen the world's perspective, which says, "All good things… must come to an end." Yet as we wound up this glorious weekend, I preferred to proclaim, "All good things…are from our eternal God, who is the beginning and the end." Every good and perfect gift is from above.

And good things were coming from Mimi too.

COOKIES DELIVERED

Since we no longer had to bribe Caleb with sweets to meander outside, we began to monitor his sugar intake. Today's would be substantial, with homemade chocolate chip cookies hand delivered by his Mimi and Aunt Terry. They brought Caleb what Mimi knew was his favorite—along with the "sweet fellowship" only shared between a grandmother and grandson. He didn't seem to know when he'd had enough, reaching for just one more cookie as they enjoyed each other's company. This was not the day to keep him from having much of either. After all, he was being able to share them with the one who loved him greatly, and she had prepared the cookies especially for him.

Caleb was much improved since Mimi and Uncle Kim's visit during SK's birthday lunch three months earlier, when we'd also used sweets to bribe him to walk the hallways of TIRR. Walking was now his own initiative, and he slowly paraded his Mimi and aunt to Windsor's front door to extend their visit before saying good-bye. He willingly and happily posed for a group photo to declare all the good that was continuing to take place around him.

The evidence of good would return again the following afternoon from Houston with our host family's visit. How grand it was to see both Taylor and Lee as we all experienced the joy that laughter brings into a day! They most definitely agreed, having experienced Caleb's very opposite sad days at TIRR Memorial Hermann.

As smooth as the water on Lake Conroe had been the day before, today's waters were rough. The body of water was the same, but appearances on the lake were not. Even when waters are calm, there are the usual man toys present to intermittently disturb the calm, such as boats and other watercraft.

Today I watched one unusual movement I'd never seen before—over water. A helicopter hovered above the lake, attempting to rescue a person in distress. The closer the helicopter moved toward the person, the more it churned the water out in all directions from him. A lifeline then appeared and was lowered to rescue the person who grabbed hold tightly to be pulled to safety. The visual took my mind to the Spirit of God's movement that I've read about in Genesis 1:2 (NIV). "Now the earth was formless and empty, darkness was over the surface of the deep, and the Spirit of God was hovering over the waters."

We continued to see the Holy Spirit's activity and to experience His power in our midst. Grasping ever so tightly, we were enjoying this part of the journey, believing that we were being pulled closer and closer to Him. This revelation to hold on tight would come up again during the team meeting with Dr. Cassidy the next day—except we wouldn't be in attendance.

WE MISSED THE MEETING!

"Somebody has to pay!" would've been my typical response to not being given the revised meeting time with Dr. Cassidy and the "team." Fortunately, the One who has paid the price for all had worked out a significantly better plan before Kurt and I had the opportunity to conduct our own non-glorifying transaction.

Dr. Cassidy was hurriedly approaching his car with briefcase in hand when we arrived for our consultation. He had other appointments scheduled, but he did allow Kurt a brief intercept to ask some specific questions while standing in the parking lot. The divine opportunity came in being able to continue our meeting before the rest of the team departed from the conference room, enjoying a much more comfortable visit without the normal time constraints.

Time was a major topic of discussion when it came to Caleb's surge of progress after clearing PTA. The decision was made that Caleb would no longer require twenty-four-hour watch and would only have a caregiver during the hours requiring therapy. It would be a bold-faced lie to say we had no fear upon hearing their unanimous opinions, even while reconciling the blessing hidden within this change.

Caleb continued on the topic of time during our afternoon and evening visit. It was fun to hear Caleb say over dinner, "You know what one of the blessings of all this is? I am excited to be spending time with y'all, but if I had spent this much time with you when I was in College Station, it would have been annoying." That was both a blessing and the truth.

Recognizing self—God's designed DNA that distinguishes who we each are individually, or in Caleb's case, trying to regain the essential qualities of who he was—is the mystery that comes with recovering from a brain injury. With self-awareness comes introspection, and Caleb began wondering if people would recognize that he had been injured. We had hoped for these difficult days when his memory would begin holding on to his conscious thoughts, and we encouraged him to work out his memory just as he would a muscle—and not worry. Kurt challenged him to cling to two words: *initiative* and *patience*.

We were all beginning to see the end of our days at Touchstone, and we needed his final ones to be put to the best possible use. Caleb took the initiative Saturday morning to shower, shave, and dress himself with little, if any, suggestion. With an approved day pass, it was his first outing outside the city limits of Conroe, Texas, and he asked to pump and pay for the gas before beginning our seventy-mile jaunt around Houston to see my parents.

Time spent visiting with doting grandparents has always been restful for Caleb, but he did take opportunities to rise from the couch and lie on the floor to execute some occasional stomach crunches throughout the day. The only obstacle holding him down each time was his big dog, Jazzy, who was excited to be at his same eye level. After several attempts to muscle off her large, wagging body, he didn't mind her lying right by his side. He hadn't remembered her previous visit at Touchstone, yet she still greeted him as if it was their first—just as tomorrow's surprise reunion with visitors would be for Caleb.

64

IGOSIANS

These natives have traveled the world over, experiencing cultures in Germany, China, Jordan, Tokyo, Africa, and Paris to carry a common message to "Make Him Famous." They surprised Caleb at Chipotle for lunch after worship services, and then they came to the house, where we watched Caleb encounter a therapy you can only get from friends and family as his memories and emotions stirred. They joined Caleb in "cooking therapy," bundling green beans wrapped in bacon and drenched with melted butter and brown sugar to complement a wonderful supper. Igosians are such great guests and always enjoy a great meal, especially since they're trained to eat almost anything and like it, or at least pretend to.

Once Cabe's friends had hugged him and said good-bye, they headed north to Dallas, Texas, and he headed straight to the couch to rest. His brain had been run through the gauntlet, and it was tired. It was at moments like these when fears and doubts crept in, and we encouraged him to rest and not dwell on his thoughts anymore. Fatigue would be a constant reminder to measure his activities throughout his recovery—something most people can relate to even without a brain injury.

In spite of Caleb's tiredness, Kurt did test him to see if he still clung to the two assigned words. He cited them without hesitation, and we all requested prayers for us to personally put them into appropriate action. Patience was probably most needed at this point for Kurt and me as we sought Caleb's best therapy beyond Touchstone. We would also consider Sarah Kate and the sacrifices she had made for the past six months. This upcoming week she would enjoy a break from our normal routine and attend a Vacation Bible School in the local area with children her own age.

65

WHEN THE LIGHTS GO OUT

Caleb initiated a new relationship with another young resident new to the Touchstone recovery scene. His name was Jesus, and since his family visited only once a week, Caleb attempted to persuade him to join in the other house activities outside of therapy. It was good timing to have a new friend to spend time with, since the majority of their next day was spent in the dark.

Caleb and the residents were gathered in the living room at Windsor House awaiting a large pizza delivery when I arrived. Power to all the homes had been knocked out since midday after strong winds blew through the area. The tempest had been violent. I personally witnessed downed signs, trees across roadways, roofs fallen on cars, and slow-moving traffic as I prayed my way toward The Woodlands, Texas, normally a twenty-minute drive away.

I was delivering Sarah Kate to stay with my friend Ellen for the evening, and her visit turned into a sleepover due to weather I hadn't anticipated. Pulling onto the grounds of Touchstone, the storm's strength was evident. Toppled trees littering the roadway had already been moved aside to allow cars to enter and exit.

Without power, and with little else to do, most residents had already retreated to their unlit rooms for an early bedtime. Caleb and a few residents were still up, sitting in the dark, listening to his phone's playlist as long as his battery charge allowed. Spending the evening in the dark was quite enjoyable as they laughed with caregivers at some of Cabe's song selections, only then to hear him sing most of the lyrics right along with them.

I left him in good hands as generators rolled into Touchstone on big trucks to light the homes—and oh, how I wished it could've been the same at my home away from home. Met with stark silence and darkness, it was a dramatic scene that I wasn't even accustomed to watching on TV. I was also dependent on electricity for many things, from powering my communication devices to calming my frizzy hair each morning.

Walking through the duplex, holding a single light from my phone to guide me, I searched for the gift of this night. Though many lights constantly shine in our lives, and numerous noises always surround them, I was now forced to follow only one light as it shone down on the silent carpeted path from the den to the bedroom. God spoke to me in my thoughts: "I am your source of light and will lead you in the way I want you to go. Listen for me and tune out the other noises of the world."

When you only have one source of light, it will keep you focused on moving in the right direction. After resting well, with the storms gone from the area, I left the next morning to retrieve Sarah, hoping that when I returned to the house there would be power.

66

FUZZY WAS HE

Fuzzy-face Caleb greeted me in the afternoon with a list of three things he wanted to talk about. Before he shared his list, I asked him if anyone had told him to shave. He said no, and then went on to tell me he wanted to grow a beard. A beard wasn't part of the exit plan, and shaving himself was. So I found it easy to tell him so. His written list revealed his readiness to move to outpatient therapy, which brought up his question: "Will I always have to write things down to remember?" I couldn't honestly answer that question, but can I tell you I wouldn't remember much of what I am writing today had I not written it down. Whether it's to help with memory loss or for the sake of others who come behind, the written word is definitely a gift.

A brief break from Touchstone's premises to Chrissie and Jimmy's home to pick up SK gave me the opportunity to also stop and load up on packaged ice cream cones for the caregivers and residents. Sarah always enjoyed giving out the treats, and Caleb was nowhere to be found in the living area when we arrived. So before handing out the cones, she went to roust Caleb from his room.

I couldn't have been prouder of him had he posted a 4.0 grade average in college. When he entered the room, it was obvious Cabe had remembered to take the initiative and had seized a few moments during my intermission. He was clean-shaven, except for a couple of missed patches, and for this endeavor he received a double portion. I recalled the scripture in a CaringBridge entry: "Instead of your shame you will receive a double portion, and instead of disgrace you will rejoice in your inheritance. And so you will inherit a double portion in your land, and everlasting joy will be yours" (Isaiah 61:7 NIV).

Caleb took advantage of the rewards-based initiative program before him, telling me how he also thought a puppy would bolster his recovery. I laughed because he's requested a four-legged companion ever since leaving home for college. We'd stick to ice cream. Sarah Kate and I told him good night and found a room in Conroe when we realized we were still powerless at our place of rest.

The next day Caleb showed me the different lists he had created between therapies. He'd written as many characteristics of God as he could, starting with each letter of the alphabet. He produced additional lists for names of friends, cities in the United States, foods, and things most folks would like to have. It was a fun activity allowing Sarah Kate to participate as well. When reading his list of "things I would like to have," the letter A stood for "Alaskan husky." Definitely a declaration of evidence that Caleb's retention was increasing and his selective memory was faring well. This was a great exercise and a reminder. I should've made my own list of things to be thankful for. At this point, the return of electricity was a highlight, as was Kurt's safe arrival after traveling over eight hundred miles in less than a week. We were glad he'd be here for his extended birthday weekend, and Caleb was determined to grill steaks to perfection for him.

Kurt picked Cabe up on Sunday morning, and both men shopped for groceries as a team. It's amazing just how many groceries two men can walk through the doors with, and how taxing this therapy can be even for those without a brain injury! After unloading the groceries (my job), we went to church, and Caleb knew all but one of the songs sung. It became his favorite over the upcoming months after its recent release and growing popularity. "10,000 Reasons" would also become the background music for a recovery video six months in the future. Until then, the song for the day was one that Caleb and everyone knows very well: "Happy Birthday." It was yet one more reason for a pass to leave Touchstone, this time on a weekday.

We headed south of Conroe to an area where restaurants are plentiful and celebrations are a daily happening. We were formally celebrating Kurt's birthday and Caleb's gains in recovery since my birthday. From my chocolate cake celebration at St. Anthony's in January to seafood at Pappadeaux's in June, we thought "10,000 Reasons" might be the more appropriate song to sing. Of course, we found so fitting the first sentence of *Jesus Calling* for the day, which read, "I AM THE FIRM FOUNDATION on which you can dance and sing and celebrate My Presence."

After eating so much food, we didn't feel much like dancing on a full stomach, but we did take a walk, completing over a half mile at a nearby park. We returned to Touchstone for a happy reprisal and birthday cake with the residents and caregivers. Then we told Caleb that we'd see him at five o'clock tomorrow. "Feel free to come back sooner" was his reply. I don't think he wanted to be left behind for fear that he might miss something else after all the celebrating.

Caleb probably thought so again the next day when I asked him if he knew what day it was. Laughingly relieved he hadn't forgotten some other special occasion, he remembered today was only "hump" day, and another weekend was right around the corner. We all found a rekindled humor in the redundant phrase posed by Sarah Kate (in her given voice) to Caleb (and everyone else within hearing range) *every* Wednesday—for a year before Geico made its "hump day" camel famous. Our laughter went even further a year and a half later when the Geico camel himself proclaimed—via a New Year's Eve Tweet on national television—that he and Caleb had more than just the previous year in common. Who knew the humped quadruped was also named Caleb?

Kurt left for Victoria on Wednesday, and I left on "hump day" plus one, as Sarah Kate referred to Thursdays. Physically checking out facilities for Caleb's post-Touchstone phase of recovery would be our next steps over the coming days, after Kurt tackled the discussion of a release date with Dr. Cassidy during his long drive home.

As Caleb quizzed me Wednesday evening about when and where Kurt and I had first met, Kurt's call interrupted the exam to say he'd gotten home safely. He was delighted to tell Caleb that Touchstone's departure date had been negotiated for June 26, with a layover in Houston to repair his eye before heading home.

Leaving very early the next morning toward Victoria, Conroe disappeared in my rearview mirror as I glanced over Sarah Kate's head. This was the first time that Kurt and I would both be away from Caleb for a twenty-four-hour period in five and a half months. Cindy and KK welcomed the invitation to be our replacements, and Caleb didn't have any reservations whatsoever with that solution. He was glad to be able to personally share the good news with them, and the thought of going *home* made him beam as he spoke about it.

The light was growing brighter at the end of this tunnel, and Caleb's eyes were focused on reaching it. Our conference call would soon take place with Dr. Cassidy to discuss Caleb's best exit strategy so we would be ready once the day came. We were all excited!

67

CDJ

About twenty miles east of Victoria, I received a God-wink that made me smile big for the remaining minutes driving toward home. The car directly ahead of me to the right was sporting a non-customized Texas license plate ending with the three letters CDJ, Caleb's initials. I couldn't begin to imagine how long I might have looked had I been searching the highways (as we often still do on long family trips) for a license plate with his initials. Yet I didn't have to. The Lord was reminding me that He had gone before me in search of outpatient facilities. And He had.

Kurt and I visited the Victoria rehab facility and left there, not in awe of Warm Springs (though it was wonderful) but in awe of God. As we sat and listened to the therapists explain their areas of expertise, we were pleased with what we heard. We shared Caleb's experiences with his previous therapists and his advances made thus far. We also took the opportunity to speak out about our faith in God and His provisions after choosing Caleb for this journey.

With eyes glassing over and lips quivering, two therapists acknowledged that they had already been praying for Caleb during a Thursday evening Bible study group. We found it no coincidence; their study was on miracles. I cry when I recall this moment in time, knowing God orchestrated everything for all who could see. I thank Him today, as I did that day in June, for showing us how much He loves us. My response is still what it was when I wrote in CaringBridge, "I love you too, Orchestrator!"

Thursday evening, we heard a *very* tired Caleb on the phone—for several reasons. One was his big-box therapy shopping at Walmart for ingredients to help Ms. Debra prepare a Touchstone meal for the Windsor residents. Another was visiting with his cousin Ryan, who is five months older. There's no doubt they spent a lot of time talking and laughing with each other. When those two are in a room together, laughter is always plentiful and most likely targeted toward anyone who happens to be in the vicinity. Caleb also admitted to conspiring on an escape plan. We were relieved to know that he was headed toward his bed instead, and the two were not cruising down Highway 105 toward College Station— though we prayed he'd be going back there in days to come.

Kurt and I spent our first night back in Victoria together since leaving in January. The drive back to Conroe tomorrow would include a couple of predetermined stops across Houston before our round trip was completed. As I sat on the familiar corner of my couch where I read my Bible from each morning, I thought about my 2011 challenge when Pastor Tim encouraged us to read through the Bible chronologically in a year, something I had never accomplished before. In hindsight I believe it was preparation for what filled our days ahead in 2012. I was thankful for a pastor who led his sheep to waters that do not run dry. As I made time to sit and read, I read from 2 Kings 3:17–20 (NIV), which starts by saying, "…You will see neither wind nor rain, yet this valley will be filled with water … And you will drink." It ends with, "And the land was filled with water." We were full, to say the least, when we left Victoria.

The random parking lot entering Houston was shaded with trees and served us well to climb into one car before joining a scheduled conference call with Dr. Cassidy and his team following their meeting with Caleb. Sarah Kate was given her instructions to stay quiet as we listened attentively to each team member report from around the conference room table. All agreed that Caleb was ready to be released, and his discharge was still scheduled for June 26.

Best of all was hearing Dr. Cassidy tell about his visit with Caleb. He described Cabe as being relaxed, conversational, and smiling a lot. Regretfully, we couldn't see Dr. Cassidy's face, but our best guess on a visual was that he, too, was smiling from ear to ear as he described their time together. We ended the call, deciding to discuss all administrative details with Sheena upon our arrival back at Windsor House later that afternoon.

Altogether, there would be a total of three stops before we got there. A return to TIRR Memorial Hermann inpatient facility was our second, and we shared hugs with those who had served us well for forty-one days. It was with great pleasure that we told of the Lord's goodness and about the many provisions we had seen in Caleb's healing. Sarah Kate especially enjoyed the attention from her *fellow* nurses who had embraced and loved on her months before.

Our visit to a TIRR outpatient facility was the last of our stops before returning to Conroe, and we observed many patients enduring various stages of rehab. We saw state-of-the-art equipment and were given an extensive tour of the facilities. There was no doubt that TIRR was the "Cadillac" facility of outpatient rehabilitation, and we now had the daunting task of deciding where Caleb would relocate next for therapies. Both TIRR and Warm Springs charged us to consider what was best for both Caleb and our family. We began to write down the strengths and weaknesses, hoping they would enable us as we prayed to make the right decision.

Back at Windsor House, Sarah Kate darted straight toward Caleb's room, while Kurt and I met with Sheena and Caleb's case manager to discuss final paper details. Thirty minutes into finishing his exit plan, Kurt's phone rang. It was Caleb asking where we were. Kurt said that we'd just taken off from Victoria and would be at Windsor soon. Not falling for the trickery, Caleb was still very glad to see us enter his room sooner than later. Friday afternoon was here, and he knew a pass to leave Touchstone for the evening was on order. According to the newest plan, this was to be the last weekend he needed day passes, and he liked how that sounded.

Nicole was working the night-shift duty and greeted Caleb's buzz at the front door. She informed us that Caleb's friend Trey was back for a brief stay. Though both had sung in concert before, Caleb didn't remember him. We all laughed really hard when reintroductions were made and Caleb said, "Nice to meet you again." There was no iTunes song that could've sounded any sweeter than these two young men singing, "With Jesus as my Savior, a constant friend is He. His eye is on the sparrow, and I know He watches me." As the evening ended, Trey stood amazed as he watched Caleb walk away to his room by himself, because a wheelchair had only been used to take him to it the last time Trey was there.

Caleb prayed before I left that evening. He prayed for Trey. He prayed for Cade, a new teenage resident. He prayed, "Lord, protect those in the path of a brain injury right now. I pray that Touchstone will go out of business because there will not be any TBIs." I gave a resounding amen and kissed him good night.

The next day, it actually looked like a "Going Out of Business" sign should've been hung across the wing where Caleb's corner room was located. His suite mate had been released that morning, and Bill from across the hall was gone for the weekend. Caleb wasn't in his room either, as he retreated to the lake house for one final round of weekend visitors before heading home for good.

Caleb schemed to make his arriving guests believe that he wasn't expecting their visit, but he couldn't stay composed with the huge smile plastered across his face. The day was remarkable and filled to the brim with games, grilled burgers, naps, laughter, and a walk. Upon departure, all would say, "I'll see you later," but in a different location. Caleb commented to Kurt and me, "I have really good friends."

"SEE YOU LATER"

Being our final Sunday in Conroe for a while, Caleb, Kurt, and I worshipped with the April Sound Church congregation—one last time. Sarah left the day before to go to Wimberley with Aunt Cindy as preparations began for our next transition. She said, "I'll see you later," to her precious friend Riley, the God-gift whom she treasured. It was a sure first sign that leaving wasn't going to be easy for any of us.

Tears accompanied our return to the church in the afternoon to fill "care" boxes for the men and women serving our country, right alongside April Sound's church members, who did this often. Caleb walked slowly around the tables, filling each box with sundry items, choosing carefully what he placed into each one. He then, the best he could, wrote a personal note thanking each person for his dedication and service. It was wonderful therapy, both physically and emotionally, and we titled it "serving therapy."

Kurt left for a quick trip to Victoria after telling many at the church, "See you later," and Caleb and I made our way to the house to rest before "brinner" at IHOP and then on to our final stop at Touchstone. Caleb made the connection that he wouldn't be returning to the lake house again before leaving Touchstone, confirming our feelings when he declared that the house had been a wonderful blessing to Kurt and me.

As our tires hit the driveway at Touchstone, Caleb proclaimed, "This will be my last time to ride into Touchstone." I gave thanks that he'd never fought us about going back to Windsor House after having him out on passes. The extreme resistance we had experienced upon first arriving in March was no longer with him, and we had all witnessed the healing within Caleb, just as Trey had testified the night before. Trey greeted him with a big hug when Caleb walked through Windsor House's secured front door for the last time on a Sunday night. Caleb wouldn't see some of the caregivers before his Tuesday discharge because of scheduled shift changes, so he sincerely thanked them, hugged them, and promised them that he, too, would "see you later."

I can't really tell you what happened on Caleb's last day of therapy at Touchstone. I can tell you I was at the lake house packing and once again wondering how in the world we could've accumulated so much stuff over such a short period of time. There were lots of good-byes to be said, and promises from Caleb that he'd return as a visitor. In the midst of Caleb doing so, Kurt got back into town just as he was beginning to serve unhealthy portions of red velvet ice cream to the staff and patients. The attentive nurse's objection was quickly overruled. Caleb soon announced his readiness to retire to his bed for the last time, wanting to be rested for the brand new day ahead.

So, before carrying most of Caleb's things from his room to the car, Kurt and I stopped and tearfully hugged the night staff good-bye. The tears of pain from March 13 were now tears mixed with sadness and joy. We assured each one that we'd return and would be faithful to pray for them in days ahead. Jeremiah 31:13 (ESV) rang true to us: "…I will turn their mourning into joy; I will comfort them, and give them gladness for sorrow."

Our son, who had been wheeled into Touchstone and had stayed there against his wishes on that March day, was now going to walk out tomorrow to follow the One who had led him there in the first place.

As tears ran down my cheeks and fell to the page I was gripping, I tried my best to convey just how much they had meant to us. With my voice trembling I read my poem.

Windsor House, 2012

> Could you hear my heart break as we first drove away,
> Leaving here our loved one and longing just to stay?
> Your words, they held no meaning when you assured us
>   of his care.
> We prayed, "Somehow, some way, dear God, we cannot
>   leave him there."
>
> Knowing we had no choice but here, tears streamed down
>   my face,
> And I knew within my spirit, God had brought us to this
>   place.

A building that's called Windsor on the grounds known
    as Touchstone
God has held this child of mine and made this house our
    home.

It wasn't instantaneous; I fought it with all I had.
Yet each day I was softened and wasn't quite as mad.
Many of you told us you have prayed for us each day,
And when presenting your gift to Father God—your
    service is your pay.

You rubbed his feet, scratched his back, and still he hit
    on you.
You redirected his behavior in the loving way you do.
The aggression stage soon ended, and you spoke blessings
    to our son.
You encouraged him to rise up, and applauded when he
    chose to run.

You fixed the snacks he asked for and read to him from
    Jesus Calling.
You kept him clean, pushed his chair, and steadied him
    from falling.
You have listened to a complaining mom and a dad way
    too concerned.
You have loved our family as your own and been patient
    as we've learned.

So our hearts are full of joy today, but sadness lingers too
As we try our best to express in words our many thanks
    to you.

Just as our God in heaven loves in spite of all our sin,
You've gone the second mile with us, time and time again.

So to all who work at Windsor House, we pray God's favor rests on you,
And you'll continue to show who Jesus is through every task you do.
That each patient passing through here will know what we have known:
Windsor is Beyond the Best ... Our home here at Touchstone.

—The Jentsch Family

Caleb Jentsch was a resident at Touchstone's Windsor House, March 13–June 26, 2012, due to a skiing injury (TBI) in January, 2012.

"LORD, I have heard of your fame; I stand in awe of your deeds, LORD. Repeat them in our day, in our time make them known; in wrath remember mercy" (Habakkuk 3:2 NIV).

www.caringbridge.org/visit/calebjentsch

69

WELCOME HOME ... SOON

We didn't go directly home when we left the Conroe area. In fact, Kurt and Caleb left before I did for his pre-surgery eye exam to make certain the surgery scheduled for the following day was still a go. I stayed behind for last-minute condo cleaning, determined to leave it in the same good condition in which we had found it. I resisted the temptation to turn backward the Longhorn-etched stone on the fireplace hearth, as is the habit of Aggies in our immediate family. It just didn't seem right after being so blessed to call this place home for the past three months. I would choose the greater good. After the off-white carpets were cleaned and I'd closed the white metal door for the last time, I looked out over the lake and thanked God for this perfect provision during our time of need, and for once again preparing the way before us.

Driving out of the now familiar neighborhood, I waved good-bye to the security guards and looked in my rearview mirror to make sure the fully packed car allowed my vision a clear path. I drove the same roads that had led me here from Houston in March, only this time in the opposite direction and without the need for a snack. We were welcomed back to the Wedgeworths' home again, gaining access the moment we arrived with the key we were allowed to keep.

Caleb met the parents of one of his best Aggie friends after their workday ended, even though the Wedgeworths had already met him several times at TIRR and Touchstone. These reintroductions and their accompanied stories were significant to reconstructing the days of Caleb's life that he would never remember on his own. Fortunately, their stories were mostly enjoyable, except for mentioning times when Caleb was agitated and depressed. He showed no sign of either now, and only feared the anticipated pain looming over the planned eye surgery. Caleb's nervousness for tomorrow was apparent, and he made a wise choice to participate in games after we all ate pizza. His anxiety eased, and he slept well in what we all labeled the softest (and Sarah Kate's favorite) bed in the house.

We arrived at the hospital as instructed at 9:15 a.m., and Caleb was prepped and looked ready with a big X marked above his right eye. Before leaving the surgical area, Kurt and I prayed with Caleb and his surgeon. The three hours of waiting passed quickly, and it was great to hear a one-eye-patched Caleb say post-surgery, "I didn't feel a thing. We serve an awesome God." We agreed. It didn't take twenty-twenty vision to see that.

As we wheeled Caleb to the car, a Rice Krispies Treat and some juice helped ease his hunger pangs after having been denied a presurgery breakfast. Back at the Wedgeworths' he napped all afternoon and experienced no pain. We then enjoyed our final meal and evening with the Wedgeworths and telling them goodbye. Our last stop in Houston would be a midmorning follow-up to reveal the results of Cabe's surgery—and then we would go home.

RETURN TO YOUR OWN LAND

The doctor certified that all had gone remarkably well, so we put both cars on cruise control and headed home, a place Caleb hadn't been in 2012. The verse from Ezekiel 37:14 (NLT) was our voice: "I will put my Spirit in you, and you will live again and return home to your own land. Then you will know that I, the LORD, have spoken, and I have done what I said. Yes, the LORD has spoken!"

The song Caleb woke to played over and over in our minds as we traveled south down Highway 59. We sang along intermittently with the recording, as we had done a few years earlier while watching rejected American Idol contestants sing, "I'm going home to the place where I belong." We really didn't remember the lyrics except for those few words, but they were worth repeating, and Caleb sang them as his new favorite song.

The closer our two cars got to Victoria, the more at-home we felt. Just a few miles from our exit all eyes turned to three decorative poster signs on the side of the road, strategically placed several yards apart from each other. They proclaimed that our homecoming was the work of the Lord. The first was printed with marks of excitement surrounding it. It said, "The LORD is good, a refuge in times of trouble. He cares for those who trust in Him" (Nahum 1:7 NIV). The second was an encouragement from Philippians 1:6 (ASV): "being confident of this very thing, that he who began a good work in you will perfect it until the day of Jesus Christ." And the final one was from Romans, which validated the call on Caleb's life by saying that everything is for God's glory. It was so much fun to pull the car over to read the signs aloud, take a moment to snap a picture with each, and then leave them behind for others to see. The short distance to our Victoria home included a planned detour around town to Warm Springs to let Caleb view the facilities of his future. As appropriately named, we were greeted "warmly" by all.

Greater than warm was the greeting back at our house. Our home had been transformed into a welcome center! The first clue was the sight of a yellow ribbon around the old "some kind of" tree—and being handed mini-Blizzards as we drove on to the driveway. We knew what was waiting inside would be decorative, but we couldn't have imagined the messages on *every* mirror in the house, balloons in every room, fresh flowers, streamers hanging from the ceiling, snacks waiting in the fridge, more notes of encouragement, and dinner on the way. Our friends had done exceedingly, abundantly more.

Caleb reopened his rewrapped Christmas gifts, and Kurt and I celebrated the *gift* of having him home to watch him open them again. Though we missed Sarah Kate's and Eric's presence at this Christmas celebration, it seemed God had given us this time alone to enjoy His provision for Caleb. Needless to say, as I lay my head on my pillow for this long-awaited night, tears stained my pillowcase, and I thanked God for a perfect day.

July 1 was the completion of another circle in Wimberley, Texas, where we had celebrated Christmas 2011 at our "home away from home" before heading to the slopes of Colorado. It was from central Texas Caleb had left to meet friends in Dallas for a New Year's Eve celebration before beginning the long drive to Denver with the A&M ski gang a couple of days later. We read the "Welcome to Wimberley" sign by the bridge as we entered this small hill-country town, and I realized that Caleb had come full circle after six months.

The celebration awaiting us was laced with family and friends gathering around a welcome sign that shouted, "Oh Happy Day!" And indeed it was. It didn't take too long before Caleb wanted to make the walk to the beckoning river and lie in the hammock. My mind recited the Twenty-Third Psalm as I watched him. It echoed, "He leads me beside quiet waters," and "Even when I walk through the darkest valley ... you are close beside me."

Cabe's life was inching toward normalcy as best he could manage. At this juncture, markers included sparring with his seven-year-old sister, exchanging I love yous, and watching a movie together. He especially enjoyed the fried okra prepared expressly for him the first night, a banquet table he felt had been personally set for him. He again rested well in a bed he claimed as his own, and we were so pleased to see the direction his independence was now beginning to take him when not fatigued and in need of rest. He would work to serve his own cereal several times a day and then remember to put his dishes away. He even requested to prepare our dinner one evening, which consisted of the infamous "Anniversary Chicken" and green bean casserole.

Our prayers thanking God for the hands of the preparer were most sincere this night.

PARADE OF INDEPENDENCE

I'm sure many of you have heard the word picture that uses a parade to illustrate the difference in what we see and what God sees. I am a learner who requires word pictures to "get it," and this one helped. It goes something like this.

We see most things in our life as if we are watching a parade. We only see a few things that have previously passed us by in the parade (which quickly become just a memory), those that are presently holding our attention directly in front of us (which we make judgments on), and very few things yet to come (which are clearly within our scope of sight). God sees differently. He sees the whole parade, the beginning and end and everything in between. He knows where the end began, as well as what's coming into our future. In other words, *nothing* is a surprise to Him.

We were able to enjoy the Wimberley Fourth of July parade while sitting on the tailgate of Kurt's Dodge Nitro. It served as the perfect vantage point as Caleb awaited his sister's and nousin's debut, thanks to cousins with connections. (Caleb has called his cousin's daughter his *nousin* since birth, because he thinks of Ryan as a brother, making his daughter Cabe's niece.)

In the not-too-far distance was Old Baldy—what we naive Texans like to call a mountain. Caleb and Ryan recalled running up its formidable steps to the peak during many summers while attending tennis camps together in Wimberley. Kurt, overhearing them reminiscing, jokingly asked Caleb if wanted to climb (walk up 223 steps) to its summit later. Caleb instantly (and *not* jokingly) responded, "Sure, I think I can do that." We were glad *the ask* wasn't to go at that very moment, and we hoped that he'd forget about it. We certainly didn't bring it up again. We liked the things that we were now seeing directly in front of us in Caleb, but we couldn't see too far ahead. We were trusting in the one and only God who sees all, trying not to anticipate what was coming down the road for Cabe—or for us, for that matter.

While in Wimberley, Caleb continued daily sessions of cognitive therapies, completing memory worksheets as I produced them. Occupational therapy was limited to completing his activities of daily living, and physical therapy was a natural occurrence while walking the terrain anywhere in Wimberley. The *best* therapy, however, came at the end of each day. It was what I like to call "porch therapy." It's the best because all that's required after a long summer's day is sitting on the back porch overlooking the green grass and the clear flowing river in the distance. Add in music provided by various birds calling to one another, and a conversation with those you love, and you've got a recipe sure to calm and soothe all your senses.

Some of Cabe's friends made trips from across Texas to see him on Saturday following the Fourth, and were quick to share the improvements and headway they saw in Caleb. The evening turned to the annual gathering of our Wimberley family and friends of families, complete with honoring this year's high school grads, a children's parade, all the barbecue fixins, and homemade ice cream. Caleb was a little anxious about the crowd, but his fears were quieted once he stepped into the yard of familiarity, escorted by his cousins and friends. He did well socially and celebrated from seven to ten p.m., causing him to be extremely tired when he went to bed at eleven.

In his admitted weariness, he asked me, "Do you ever wonder why God didn't just take me, because I would be in heaven with him?" I could honestly answer no. I believed, and still believe, that God sees what's coming up ahead in the parade, and it is something special for Caleb. He was tired enough that he didn't dwell on the question or my answer and instead went on to sleep. He rested much of the next day, which would be needed for his planned days of therapies lying ahead next week.

So we tightly packed our car along with extra passengers to return home to Victoria on Sunday. Sarah Kate and Jazzy were now accompanying Kurt, Caleb, and me as we headed southeast. As I quoted from *The Wizard of Oz* and *Homeward Bound* in my updates: "There's no place like home" and "I don't care about gates. I'm going home!" After 120 miles of togetherness, we all gladly unloaded from the car on our Tanglewood driveway, and Jazzy christened the ground in approval. I wrote at the end of that day, "Thank You, Lord, for bringing us home safely and making Your home with us, wherever we have been."

72

THERAPIES AWAIT

From nine to twelve, three days a week, Caleb worked through therapies Warm Springs formatted especially for him. Friends picked up Sarah Kate to attend an all-day summer music camp every morning during our first week home, which was a blessed provision that allowed me to be at the outpatient center.

After three solid hours of mental and physical work, Caleb's response to my question, "How was therapy?" was a barely audible "Fine." He had no energy left to expound on anything, and he came home, ate, and then tried to nap. Napping proved to be mostly unsuccessful the first few days, so he would lay on the couch playing computer games, while I began unpacking four months of stuff to clear floor space in the living area. Caleb didn't seem to mind and enjoyed his time by himself. By the time Kurt arrived home from work each day, Caleb was revived and ready to play some cards and go for a walk. Suggesting that we walk to the end of the street and back the first evening, Caleb surprised us both by not looking back—walking the full block instead.

He connected well with the Warm Springs therapists and spoke often to his PT about being able to stand for long periods of time. He was looking ahead to college football games in the fall, wanting to be sure he possessed the stamina to stand the whole game with all the other Aggies representing the 12th Man. During the first weeks living at home, we were able to see other deficiencies that hadn't been visible to us while living apart from Caleb.

Executive planning/ordering was a term we'd heard many times throughout Caleb's recovery, and seeing examples now play out in his life enabled us to understand some of what he was dealing with mentally. During a trip to the grocery store for a full basket of food, I observed Caleb's ability to maneuver through the aisles of HEB while being surrounded by baskets stalled for one reason or another. It was an opportunity to see him exercise patience while making adjustments and handling the frustrations as they occurred. I must admit, Caleb wasn't the only one struggling with the indecisive basket-pushers ahead of us.

Our grocery bill was more than double what it had been, now that we were feeding a hungry college-age boy—including additional items Caleb had placed into the basket while I was distracted. On the return trip home, I agreed to carry the groceries inside if he would start putting them up. That was when the word *completion* came to my mind. Caleb was all about completing the job he'd agreed to do; putting the items in order wasn't as important. He did put the refrigerator items in the fridge and the pantry items in the pantry, but any rational arrangement was missing.

Now, I certainly don't want you to confuse me with my mother's friend who alphabetizes everything in her pantry. I only organize by shelves, and I wonder if they would ever really be considered organized or not. Yet it was evident that there was certainly no order as Caleb loaded onto one shelf as much as it could hold before moving on to another, without rhyme or reason as to where he placed the assorted goods. Regardless, I was thankful for his help, and I rearranged as necessary. I was also thankful to see the evidence of where Caleb would need our help as the days moved forward.

As his recovery continued, we were reminded that moving through a brain injury is like hitting a moving target. We found this to be very true, and we tried to stay prayerfully focused on our goal to consider the sum of the days, not any one in particular. We saw memory gains, except when Caleb was fatigued. We could only relate to the way our own minds are affected by physical tiredness. Add to the equation the fact that the mind is not only tired but also injured, and the brain seems to take a double toll when trying to complete the simplest of tasks. Medically, this has been found to be true, and it proved to be the case for our son as well.

While working a puzzle, the Lord revealed to me that my "good plans" might not be the best game plan at the present time. Caleb spied me walking through the den carrying a puzzle I'd received at Christmas and asked if he could help me put it together. I was thrilled he'd taken the bait and was so looking forward to watching his mind manage the work needed to put the irregular shapes together.

We started by sorting out the edge pieces first, which has always been the best strategy for me to start a puzzle; then you complete the framework and proceed from there. After carefully sorting out all the edges, it became apparent my method was a huge mistake. All the edges were the exact same color and would be a nearly impossible task for me, let alone Caleb, to try to complete! As I scrapped my plan to convey another, Caleb was already exiting the room, probably thinking, *I won't fall for that again.* Working the puzzle over the next few weeks, I found it to be a personal escape from the daily draws of life. It would also be the times when Caleb sat down at the table with me to look for a particular piece that I enjoyed the most. These times of unplanned activity provided both a mental exercise and time to communicate "off the record."

Mornings tended to be the best time of day for Caleb. His mind and body were both rested. Kurt would drop him off for therapies, and I would pick him up later. The mornings were full of energy: Caleb was talkative and motivated for the schedule ahead of him. When I picked him up at noon, he appeared to be a different person in the same body. His whole being showed evidence of being tired.

Not only could I see the exhaustion challenging his effort just to walk to the car, but answering the simplest of questions proved to be very difficult for him. Subsequently, Sarah Kate asked Caleb what his favorite toppings on frozen yogurt were (which she deemed as important), and he struggled to come up with an answer. We already knew his weak muscles were from a lack of use and were not injury related, as previously noted by his therapists. Lots of physical energy would be required to build them back up over time, which in turn created a fine balancing act to mentally complete both speech and occupational therapies during the same morning.

We were always encouraged after Caleb recharged during the afternoons and wanted to walk outside of the assigned therapy, which he did following one particular evening meal. He then came back inside looking for his backpack to complete his assigned homework. It was always a bonus when Caleb even remembered his homework, and his only challenge this night was working a Sudoku puzzle in ink. He needed to remember that this wasn't the best plan for anyone.

God once again revealed to me that He doesn't follow the plans of man. With Caleb's extreme fatigue during the day came fear and doubt from within. When Caleb exhibited doubts and fears, I in turn looked for help. I Googled "fatigue in brain injury patients" and found it to be one of the most common outcomes after suffering a traumatic brain injury. The fears that Caleb shared were also creeping up in me, until I sensed God's probing. I felt like He asked me, "Do you want Me to go with what the articles say, or would you like Me to do exceedingly more than you can ask, as I have said I can do in My Word?" Knowing the best choice, my fears subsided, as did Caleb's after a good night's rest. The last day of the first therapy week ended up being a good one.

73

TRUE VALUE

The final months of summer were endured with three prescribed therapies a day, scheduled three days each week. Variety came during family time spent with one another on weekends and some weeknights.

As each day progressed toward the end of the summer months, we saw Caleb progress also. He became stronger, both cognitively and physically. He required less assistance, and I didn't see the need to *hover* over him as much. Though follow-up visits with Dr. Cassidy were encouraging as he witnessed the positives, he wouldn't adorn Caleb with the news he longed to hear. Caleb would not be able to drive anytime soon, and he was not going to be able to return to Texas A&M University in the fall. Kurt and I were already there on both decisions, and Caleb was disappointed he couldn't drive.

Even though Caleb resolved that returning to school in the fall wouldn't be a good decision, it saddened him. Most of his friends were returning to College Station early to begin preparations for the Impact Camp. Caleb too would have been serving at this

Christian camp designed to help facilitate the needs of incoming freshman at A&M.

I also felt the sting of disappointment after Caleb and I spent a few days in College Station, seeing his friends before the semester started. I was glad Caleb's eyes were closed and Sarah Kate was engrossed in a movie to pass her time on the way to our next destination. The tears rolled continually down my face, and I couldn't stop them. My heart was crying out, "This is not fair." A simple, personal lesson learned months earlier helped me cope and understand the fair value of what we were going through.

Focusing on tough circumstances instead of on God will always create thoughts of unfairness. When struggling to fall asleep one night, God told me in my thoughts to get up and go look at a coin. Not knowing why, I did. I pulled out a random *Wyoming* quarter from our old cookie jar, and one side stated that it was the Equality State. The other side of the coin revealed its value of twenty-five cents. Not sure if this was just the way new coins were being minted, I dug out an old penny and saw its value written on one side and a picture of Abe Lincoln on the other. Both coins had revealed their values only on one side.

I tested one more by looking at a dime, which also proved to be the same. I didn't look at any more coins at 2:47 a.m. I just began listening to what was being inserted in my thoughts: "You can choose which side of the coin to look at, but only one side has My value written on it." I could focus on either the circumstances in our journey or the value of our journey. If I chose to look at our circumstances, then I definitely could not see the true value written underneath.

I also realized neutrality wasn't an option I could rest in. When attempting to view both sides simultaneously, I could only see an edge. It would have to be once more a conscious choice to turn and see the true value of this journey. And at this time of the morning especially, it made good "cents."

74

PUZZLEMANIA

The incomplete puzzle still sat in the living area when my parents came to visit. The center part of the puzzle was all that was left to complete. It was bright pink and concealed a message written in black ink. There were numerous pieces in this section, and with only two colors, it proved to be nearly as difficult as the framework itself. Friends had helped me place a few puzzle pieces while drinking coffee and visiting over the past month. My daddy sat down this evening and tried to contribute as well.

As we surrounded the puzzle, Caleb asked, "Can I put the last piece in?" to which I responded, "Yes, of course you can." Sarah Kate bounced into the room, wanting to be in the company of all, and asked, "Oh, oh, can I put in the last piece of the puzzle?" Again my response was, "Of course you can." I'd just work out the details later. Daddy and Caleb, tired of trying, headed off to bed, while Sarah went back to the den.

The puzzle, like a good dessert, kept drawing me back for just one more piece ... then one more ... and one more. Down to the final three, I slipped one piece in my pocket and called to Sarah

Kate, offering her the other two pieces on the table. She popped both into their appropriate spaces, and I told her we'd look for the remaining piece the next morning. I eased into Caleb's dark room where he was still awake, and slipped the last one into his hand.

Realizing what I was giving him, he rolled out of bed and walked the short hallway to push the final piece into place. At the jigsaw puzzle's center, the ironic message was completely revealed: "Pretending to be a Normal Person day after day can be exhausting." I said a loud amen to that and then pondered the lessons of the puzzle in relation to Caleb's injury and healing.

- Some parts are easier than others.
- A framework has to be in place.
- Each piece leads to another and reveals more about what is to come and what has already happened.
- Sometimes the middle part is the hardest and takes the longest.
- People will pass in and out of your life to help.
- Your Dad, both earthly and heavenly, enjoy just sitting at the table with you.
- You are closer to completion than you realize.
- You will be handed the final piece to put in place and there will be a message for all to see.
- When it is finished, it will have been worth all your time to see the full picture of what God has done.
- The sum of the parts makes a whole.

We continued to see parts of the whole each day.

At Caleb's late-August visit to see his local eye doctor, she told us that her two young boys had prayed faithfully for Caleb and his healing over the past eight months. He was so pleased to meet them both and thank them personally for where he was today. Dr. Oakley was loving and patient when Caleb read the eye chart and asked if she would mind displaying a particular chart one more time. Her response was so Christlike. "I have all day!"

Caleb left with hopes of seeing things more clearly, and this part of the day couldn't have started any better. The new glasses provided improved sight for reading and distance, and they helped him write a CaringBridge entry while I retreated out of town for a few nights. Caleb's improved vision also provided a new therapy that he found quite enjoyable after supper—and beneficial for his days beyond Victoria.

The lanes were perfect for three who don't bowl much, and it was the first time Caleb, SK, and Kurt had ever tied up tricolored shoes together. It wasn't so much about the pins that didn't fall as it was about watching Caleb's determination to carry the ball and maintain his balance to get it to them. Add in a natural-born cheerleader with brother's every step, and you've got enough strength and endurance to make it through any ten frames! Needless to say, they enjoyed their time without me, and I enjoyed my time away.

75

CONFESSION AND GRACE

Sarah Kate began a new school year as most of Caleb's friends were starting another new semester at A&M. It was part of the reason Caleb was down in spirit. He sat sullen. He'd had hopes (as we had) of returning to school quickly, being able to miss only one semester like his TBI brother Pierce had.

It had been exactly a year ago when Caleb called home crying and asked us to pray for a college freshman in his Impact group. Pierce had returned home for a long weekend and had been severely injured during a skateboarding accident. Though the two young men had the common ground of a traumatic brain injury, the roads to their individual recovery looked very different. Their common ground was in who was leading them: their consistent, promise-keeping God, who had led Pierce and his father to Colorado in the beginning.

We continually encouraged Caleb when he was met with delays, reminding him to trust the God who was writing the story on the pages of his life. Caleb told Dr. Cassidy a few days later that things were going well, just not as fast as he would like. Dr. Cassidy,

Kurt, and I, and all those following Caleb's journey, understood his words all too well. We had all experienced times in our lives when we desired things to go faster than they were.

Kurt and I even tried to help speed things along, confessing to Dr. Cassidy that we had begun cutting back on one of Caleb's meds we knew he was planning to reduce. Dr. Cassidy was not pleased with our action, but he handled us well. He did not spring from his chair and come hug us and say, "Thank you for taking over for me." He also didn't rise up angrily out of his chair and come bust us upside the head while saying, "How could you be so stupid to think you know more than I do." He simply looked at us and calmly said, "I wish you hadn't done that." He had a plan of action, and we had moved ahead faster than he would have liked to.

When asked if we should add the cut dosage back, he said, "No, we will adjust to where we are now and move forward from here." That was such a real-life example of how God deals with us at times when we move ahead with our plans and don't wait for His course of action. He doesn't affirm our decisions, nor does He condemn them. He doesn't work backward but moves forward from where we are. He gently talks to us about *His* plan and hopes we will choose to walk in it.

Dr. Cassidy had devised a very strategic one to move Caleb along a prescribed path so he wouldn't return to the place of agony where he'd seen Caleb for many months during the spring. His plan was not moving along as quickly as we liked, but after rational thinking, we agreed. The doctor of neuropsychiatry who had treated numerous brain injury patients before Caleb, who had written books about the brain, which many doctors referred to, and who continued to learn all he could about the brain and it's healing—knew best.

I was reminded of how often I've questioned God's timing, so easily forgetting about His *numerous* experiences with mankind, the *Book He has written*, which has been referred to for years, and His *continuous love* for a broken world.

76

CHANGE OF SEASONS

Though the seasons hadn't changed from summer to fall yet, it seemed something had changed with the start of a new school year. Football season had started, hurricane season was upon us, and the hope for a slight cool front was anticipated.

It was on a stifling, hot evening that we waited until seven o'clock to make a second attempt at driveway badminton, which didn't include the net. There was a marked difference in Caleb's attempts from the day before when he stood solely in one spot while Kurt or I tried to deliver the shuttlecock directly to him. Today, cued by Roger that Cabe was working on lateral movements in PT, Kurt positioned a shot just outside of his reach, luring him to take a step in our predetermined direction.

At first Caleb's lack of confidence kept his feet planted, but competitiveness prevailed. His boldness soared, and he continued to step further and further to reach each shot. It was such a good time, and oh, how I wished there'd been a grandstand of applause erupting each time he swung and hit!

The applause would have followed Caleb indoors and settled all around him as we both attempted to play *Tetris* on the Wii. It is an old but timely video game that requires fitting geometrically odd-shaped pieces into strategic positions as the game's speed increases. Caleb followed my turn after I did amazingly well for someone who hadn't played the game in many years. Pride cometh before the fall, and the fall came quickly as Caleb doubled my score on his first go round! Only minutes before I had feared asking Caleb to play this game, not wanting him to be discouraged and feel defeated. But my fears were for naught as they had been so many times before.

I wondered what fear must sound like in the spirit world, and I was already elated to know that whatever the discord, the applause of heaven was drowning it out! Max Lucado's book, *The Applause of Heaven*, says, "You will see the faces that are waiting for you. You'll hear your name spoken by those who love you. And, maybe, just maybe—in the back, behind the crowds—the One who would rather die than live without you will remove his pierced hands from his heavenly robe and … Applaud."

THE NINTH MONTH

September 5 marked the first day of the ninth month since Caleb's injury. Knowing several young women nearing their babies' birth day, I looked at a baby's stage of development during the ninth month of pregnancy. What I read excited me. In addition to their lungs maturing in these final weeks, their brains were continuing to develop at a swift pace, creating more than a quarter of a million neurons every minute.

That was good reading, learning that Caleb's brain was young and could still rewire after the death of many neurons, mostly attributed to the effects of shearing and the lack of oxygen to his brain. Cognitively, Caleb was gaining ground, but we searched for additional opportunities to help create neurological pathways for those that had been destroyed. Medically speaking, Dr. Cassidy had no problem with my research and encouraged us to do so, based on our ability to also manage Caleb's prescribed therapies.

So Caleb and I headed to Houston to assess a *brain-training curriculum* to see if he qualified. The training would be in addition to Warm Springs's weekly PT, ST, and OT, and we hoped it would allow his brain to heal beyond its current pace. Caleb was excited about this new adventure, which made it a much easier decision to even consider driving the roads to Houston. As long as Caleb was willing to do his part of the work, it was a path we would be willing to travel.

I overheard Caleb and the administrator laughing a lot from the other room as I observed a brain trainer working with a client. I was fascinated by their activities, not because they were extraordinary but because they were simple tasks being used in a disciplined way to cause disciplined thinking. I also noticed that Caleb wasn't being asked to be quiet within the trainer's background noise, because his voice was adding to the self-mastery the trainer was trying to produce.

Caleb tested for ninety minutes, which he said didn't feel that long, and the administrator's excitement about the success she believed Caleb could achieve couldn't be hidden. The only drawback: Caleb would be required to participate four days a week for seventy-five minutes each day—in Houston. Living ninety plus miles away and keeping family priorities in order didn't logistically make this an option for us. Desiring so much to serve Caleb, the administrator offered to train me to work with Caleb two days a week at home, and then with their most skilled trainer the other two days in Houston.

It would be a tough go, but after Kurt's and my final decision to attempt their schedule, we started training the next week: therapy at Warm Springs, lunch, a rest, and dinner. And then Caleb and I began his initial seventy-five minutes of assigned brain training exercises at home. Asking Sarah Kate to shut the door so her

TV program couldn't filter through, I quickly told Caleb no, remembering the discipline that he needed to achieve by choosing the task over the noise. Caleb needed to remain focused on the task at hand and tune out any distractions.

It's a basic discipline that will not only serve us all well throughout life, but it's a choice I believe God also wants us to make—for His mastery. Focusing on Him will diffuse the clutter of any distraction permeating our daily decisions, if we choose to live close to Him. I still find myself choosing often to turn up the noise on many occasions while tuning out His voice. It's a discipline I needed to learn well. I too would need to train my brain.

Caleb met Carol for his first on-sight training, and then Caleb wanted to continue where they had left off as soon as we returned home. I was pleased to overhear Carol speak to Caleb about self-awareness. I didn't know incorporating this tidbit came along with the LearningRx exercises, but it really did make perfect sense to me. She told Caleb to work at recognizing his forward progress without looking to others to always tell him.

Their conversation was timely in light of Caleb's concerns the night before. He had been unusually melancholy before going to sleep, and when I'd asked him why, he'd replied, "I'm not good at anything." His overall conclusion came from his inability to strike a volleyball the way he had done previously during time spent playing college intramurals. Though still better than I could ever do, his comparison was only to his pre-injury ability. He was encouraged to look forward and see the progress he was now making after only six months.

Caleb enjoyed working on brain training so much, I texted Carol to let her know how much he relished his homework away from Houston—and to thank her for the same commitment. Her reply came as if I'd received a message straight from heaven.

> I am certain it's a God-thing, that He led you to our center. I was vacationing in Wyoming [wink … remember … I had pulled out a Wyoming coin to see its value] when told about you guys. I am a born-again Christian, and I pray for all my students. My husband and I began praying for your son as soon as I heard about him. I have known for five years that God has me there for a reason, and Caleb is one of them … I finally surrendered this past year and told God I would do whatever he wanted me to do … Just show me … He has sent me some awesome students like your son. I am excited and honored to work with Caleb, as I believe God has prepared me for such a time as this! I will do everything in my power, with God's help, to help Caleb be the best he can be!

After reading her text, I could only stop and thank God once again for truly providing whom and what we needed for this time and place.

ANOTHER WEEKEND RETREAT

The weekend provided another quick getaway, but not for me this time. Caleb came home from prescribed therapies on Thursday and asked if he could go with a friend to College Station on Friday. I was confused since we'd all just gone to the season-opening football game the weekend before, and I knew the Aggies were traveling to Dallas this week to play. Caleb quickly informed us that we had remembered correctly, but many of his closest friends were receiving their Aggie rings on Saturday, and he wanted to join in their celebrations. We consented, though we were certainly torn inside about our decision to let him go. We feared how he might feel, because he too would have been celebrating personally had he not been injured.

Blessing upon blessing arrived as numerous texts flowed in from his friends with words of acclamation: "Caleb looks so good," "God is good," "Caleb smiled the whole time," and "Your son is cracking me up." Once again, Kurt and I humbly found peace and assurance despite our initial fear in letting him go. We also gave thanks for seeing the larger opportunity. We would now begin talking to Caleb about all he needed to be able to do before returning to college, along with the daily decisions that he would need to make for himself once he got there.

When I texted the following morning to see if he was awake, he texted back, "Yes, and I have already taken my meds." I also laughed at Caleb's posted reply to me after I commented on his Facebook status: "It's kinda a bummer I don't get my *wring* today, but congrats to y'all who do."

My comment brought attention to his misspelling to which he replied, "We spell it that way in Aggieland. It's a new army kind of thing." He was correct. He was part of what old Aggies call "new army." Kurt and I too had been part of Texas A&M's "new army" at one time in our lives. We had moved up the former student ranks and recognized (sometimes begrudgingly) the changes that those much younger were making to the traditions we held so dear.

This was one weekend when I thought "new army" was at its best. They reached out and cared for Caleb in numerous ways and included him in their revelry. He loved being a part of what he was missing, and we celebrated the fact that he was able to do so. It was a great trial run away from home, out from under the watchful eye of Mom and Dad for his first time.

Life continued, and Caleb returned from A&M heavyhearted, seeing his life there move forward without him. He was heartsick when the hour came to leave College Station and he couldn't stay and be a part of it. The silver lining was Caleb's ability to recognize that he wasn't ready to stay behind, even though he wanted to. It was a time to reach out once again to those who had prayed for Caleb, asking for prayer that he be content to enjoy God's provisions where he was in life at this time.

After the round trip home, his spirit was lifted when he attended an evening Bible study at the local Baptist Student Ministry. It provided a refreshing start to a new week.

HOUSTON, THE NOT-SO-BIG CITY

Our travels took us up and down Highway 59 to Houston weekly for brain-training activities, with scheduled monthly visits with Dr. Cassidy in between. Some milestones that we often encountered wouldn't appear to most as being mountain-moving events. As usual, Dr. Cassidy engaged Caleb in conversation about his life since their last visit, and then Caleb challenged him to a brain-training activity that he had conquered. Caleb was always the joyful victor. His doctor was more than proud of an adopted son, which we saw Caleb becoming to him.

Dr. C continued his plan of action, completely eliminating one medicine that Caleb had taken since March. Caleb would no longer be taking meds three times a day, but only two, and he gladly changed the alarm reminder on his phone. After watching Caleb swallow numerous pills three times a day for seven and a half months, Kurt and I saw this as movement of the mountain. And on this mountainous journey, we gave thanks at every good movement we observed.

In the big city of Houston, Texas, Caleb and I usually ate lunch at a favorite eating establishment of mine, which was less than a block away from the building housing the brain-training classes. When considering the vast number of people in Houston and the number of eating places to choose from, it seems very unlikely you will see someone you know, especially when you don't live in that area.

I was so happy to see a former student and her mother and to be greeted with such embracing hugs, only then to be told how much we had been prayed over for the last nine months. She had not only been my student, but she had also been a good friend of our son Eric and my student assistant during their senior year. She had been a treasure as an assistant, and she was now an even greater treasure as a beautiful, expectant mother professing words of encouragement to us.

Like many times during this journey, God placed people in our path so we could know it was He who was working out His plan for His good. My only response could be, "I love you too, Father!"

80

BABY ARRIVAL IN THE MAIL

Exactly nine months to the day from Caleb's injury, Baby arrived in the mail.

Kurt, Caleb, and I carefully opened the UPS package and observed her pink, soft, and unworn features. We then hid her in a drawer before Sarah Kate arrived home from school so as not to ruin the surprise planned for her. Sarah Kate would never be fooled to think that this pink stuffed bunny was her "Ella Bella" left behind in Colorado, but we knew she'd receive the replacement with love and would embrace her as if she were. The new bunny was also identical to her original baby, which we called "Hole Baby," but it was absent the holes from Sarah Kate rubbing it against her face for the first five years of her life and carrying it everywhere she went.

Unfortunately, Hole Baby too had been lost in the throng of Aggies gathered outside Kyle Field while awaiting a football game in the fall of 2009. Wisely, we had bought a backup a few years earlier, just in case her prize possession was ever lost. The replacement bunny had been graciously accepted, and SK had given her a new name. The adjustment took a while, but eventually Ella Bella became the baby of choice when choosing from her vast stuffed animal collection.

That was what had made it *extremely* difficult on January 6, 2012, when Sarah Kate had arrived at St. Anthony with her belongings—minus Ella Bella. Calls back to the condo rental company requesting help went unfulfilled; Ella was nowhere to be found during their cleanup. There had been many tearful nights in Denver, and we had no backup bunnies left to wipe the tears from Sarah's face. She had once again made an adjustment after a sweet church lady dispatched a caramel-colored bunny to her through the mail. SK had quickly accepted her and named her Peanut Butter.

eBay is great for finding almost anything if one tries hard enough. Arriving packaged with the new pink bunny was a tract, and I once again realized that this was not just any bunny, but one that God was using to send a message. The message had been preprinted by the seller and expressed appreciation for buying from their particular site. The remarks told of the greatest gift they had to offer: Jesus Christ. It went on to say, "I serve Him with loving obedience and find Him in my life, my hope, my everything. He invites you: 'Come to me all ye that labor and are heavy laden and I will give you rest.'" That was the precise message we needed to hear after what we considered to have been nine very long months.

But we didn't give Sarah the bunny on this day. She was being saved for a special time ahead.

SHOCKING

Sarah went without her baby for 275 days, and I knew exactly how many days had come and gone before the new bunny arrived at our front door. It seemed like the past days and months had been so very long ago since Caleb's traumatic injury, and we remembered that we had been correctly told that his healing would take a *long* time. I'd just had no real idea what "long" meant in the context of Caleb's recovery. In my personal experience, nine months had seemed like a long wait to have a baby, but when I compared it to a future event, e.g., Sarah's graduation from high school, I knew which was longer. It dawned on me how many times I've stood in a grocery line, thinking, "This is taking forever," when in actuality it had only required a few minutes. Perspective was key in defining "long."

As Caleb began to improve, some days definitely felt longer than others. It was at the end of one such day when Caleb expressed to me how bad his day had been, and then snapped back at me for attempting to help change his perspective. My encouragement was met with opposition, and I recognized his response as being much like my own at the end of many days.

Kurt again pointed out that Caleb's discouragement wasn't all bad. Caleb was sorting through the reality of who he was while conquering the negative thoughts that most often come during recovery from a brain injury. There were also times of daily sparring amid SK and Caleb as time with each other under one roof increased. This hadn't been uncommon between these two siblings before Caleb's injury, so it was somewhat a return to normalcy—albeit some interaction between them was actually quite shocking.

We often take for granted the brain's ability to process information needed to control bodily functions that we never consciously think about, nor can we command when we need it to. Caleb had been fitted with and was now sporting a new device strapped voluntarily below his right knee. The walk aid was designed to shock his muscle, which in turn sent a message to his brain as his right toes lifted. Technology was compensating for neurological damage in hopes that his brain would "retrain" to fire off signals back to his toes when he walked. It was calibrated for his normal stride as well as for jogging and offered several degrees of electrical "stimuli." Caleb had grown accustomed to wearing the cell-phone sized contraption at a modest setting of level 3, with 8 being the highest.

I was very surprised to see Sarah Kate allowing him to strap it onto her upper calf one afternoon, and I sternly intervened, instructing him not to move the walk aid's setting higher than level 1. Both agreed, and she was quite *moved* at feeling the initial shock before wincing at the pain. Empathy is best served after the experience, especially after realizing a triple jolt had accompanied each step her brother took. Caleb quickly reassured her that it wasn't so bad and was for his good. Just as Caleb was able to slowly tolerate increased levels of pain, his tolerance for others (including SK) and circumstances was gradually increasing.

There were many lessons to learn from this man-made device. Sometimes we just need a shock to help us do what we are not able to do alone. The Holy Spirit, our Helper, will prompt the believer to do the same, to do the unreachable—and it will always feel uncomfortable. He won't start at the highest level but rather meets us where our faith is comfortable, gradually moving us to greater heights, to do what we are purposed to do. God promised: "No test or temptation that comes your way is beyond the course of what others have had to face. All you need to remember is that God will never let you down; he'll never let you be pushed past your limit; he'll always be there to help you come through it" (1 Corinthians 10:13 MSG).

82

CELEBRATION WEEKEND

Birthdays for your children are always special. It's a time to remember they are a gift, particularly when there has been a close call with death.

We were anxious to celebrate Caleb's twenty-second birthday, and the celebrations started a few days early. Caleb would attend two scheduled brain trainings in Houston, plus an appointment with Dr. Cassidy sandwiched between the training days. While passing time sitting in the waiting area of Dr. Cassidy's offices, we saw the list of employees' birthdays within the organization.

As Diana escorted us down the very long hallway to Dr. C's corner office, Caleb took the opportunity to wish her an early happy birthday. Curious as to how he knew it was her birthday, she was as delighted as he was to know that they both shared this special day. Following a successful meeting with the doctor, Cabe was pampered with cake and balloons by his personal brain trainers after his training.

The prescribed therapies and unexpected celebrations resumed the next day back in Victoria. After finishing the last therapy of the morning with his OT, Nathan picked Caleb up and taxied him to a surprise birthday lunch at the Victoria Baptist Student Ministry. Caleb had been blessed with a full day of work and fun with friends, and Kurt and I both knew a rest would still be in order even after our 5:00 p.m. departure to College Station—for what he didn't know was awaiting him there. So I drove to let Kurt and Caleb catch a rest after such a busy week. Caleb seemed to mope a little before getting back into his nap, because he had received no requests from any of his Aggie friends to meet up with him upon his arrival.

His moping didn't last long, a fact he divulged in his personal update the next morning. He wrote, "By far one of the best birthdays ever." As previously conspired to, Caleb and Kurt went to a diversionary dinner with Caleb's appointed cousins, while others stayed behind to help me set up and decorate. Arriving back at their apartment, Caleb unknowingly sought me out and found us all waiting in the large party room adjacent to the pool. He was overcome as forty friends yelled surprise and then broke into the celebratory singing of "Happy Birthday"! What a treat it was to hear this fabulous group of unprofessional singers.

The merriment continued through the weekend, and we were honored to attend a banquet on Texas A&M University's campus for the 12th Man Kickoff Team. Many Aggies had joined with each other from across the country to raise scholarship funds for this noteworthy foundation. Over one hundred reserved dining tables had been prepared for the evening's guests, and it appeared that Kurt and I would be seated as two of Caleb's.

Former students, parents of current students, the Board of Regents, current coaches, former coaches (like Sherrill and Stallings), the governor of Texas, and football players of years gone by were all in attendance. The Who's Who of Aggie kingdom were present, and we honestly felt humbled and a little out of our element. It was when the president of Texas A&M greeted and hugged Caleb that any inhibitions faded away. Dr. Robert Loftin had been gracious enough to reach out to us during earlier past months, offering his sincere concern for Caleb on behalf of the university. It would be our first time to meet personally, but not our last.

As God would have it, Caleb also met some of the most honored attendees for the second time: the constituents from the Aggie Mom's Club in Denver, Colorado. Kurt and I told Caleb about the baskets of assorted goodies these women had delivered to the hospital the day after his injury. We were even more pleased to proclaim their faithfulness to pray for Caleb and our family in our time of need. Though this banquet hadn't been planned for this special meeting, we acknowledged the reunion as if it had been. We know God plans times of celebration through other people and events, and we thanked Him again for this one.

As this amazing weekend drew to a close, we unloaded our suitcases back in Victoria, only to begin repacking them for another God-planned celebration. I knew winter clothes needed to be included, but at the top of the "Things to Remember" list was the *pink bunny*.

THE GIFTS EXCHANGE

We packed over the next few days for a return visit to Colorado, and I reminded myself while sorting through clothes, we were packing for where we were going, not for where we had been. The temperatures in Victoria, Texas, and Denver, Colorado, differed by more than forty degrees.

I was challenged once again to remember that this earth is not my home, and the things I prepare for daily should reflect where I am going. John 14 (NLT) says, "Don't let your hearts be troubled. Trust in God, and trust also in me. There is more than enough room in my Father's home. If this were not so, would I have told you that I am going to prepare a place for you? When everything is ready, I will come and get you, so that you will always be with me where I am."

We checked our bags, and I had our boarding passes already printed. Moving slowly through security at the Austin, Texas, airport, Caleb and Kurt were carefully funneled through a line different from the one that Sarah Kate and I went through. Security didn't want Caleb passing through scanners for fear of messing up his walk-aid settings. Kurt already had the paperwork in good order to quickly show that Caleb required the device, but several TSA agents preferred to check out its unique capabilities on their own. Making certain Caleb moved through security without a hitch was our focus, and I was the only one sent back to remove my shoes.

We finally passed through the checkpoint and were boarding the plane as I overheard Caleb ask Sarah Kate, "When was the last time you flew in an airplane?" I immediately remembered the flight home from Denver with Sarah and without Kurt and Caleb. I thanked God for the gift of this return flight back, with all three now close by my side.

The touchdown at DIA felt no different this time around, but the weather would as I looked out the plane's small, double-glass window. With temperatures dropping, the cold forty-five-degree rain began to mix with snow, and we hurried from the rental car to eat in the Belmar shopping district, an area of distraction we had enjoyed while Caleb was hospitalized. The mixture had become solely snowfall by the time we finished a late supper, painting the landscape almost exactly like that first somber evening when we'd pulled into St. Anthony Hospital.

The parking lot was still spotted with cars, and Kurt stopped the car and did his best to recall the heavy events of ten months before. He then pointed slowly to Flight for Life, still perched high atop the fourth story's landing pad as our car began to ease forward. We drove slowly past the red-lit emergency sign we had walked under in January. We then circled around to the front entrance to take time to photo Caleb entering St. Anthony as a visitor. He smiled, and we smiled. It was our pleasure to show him the beautiful facility in detail: where we'd eaten, the bathrooms, the gift shop, the waiting area where his friends and family had taken over, and then the trauma ICU unit ...

Moving from the outside waiting area through the doorway and into the TICU hallway, Kurt, SK, and I were unsure what to expect. We saw no familiar faces and received no probing looks in exchange. We asked the closest nurse if Juri was on night duty and if it was okay to walk the floor.

Permission granted, we slowly walked toward the room Caleb had occupied for the month of January, and it didn't take him long to recognize the serious condition of each person occupying a space on the second floor. Caleb agreed; it was a sobering place. We continued moving quietly through several hallways, casting looks and smiles toward nurses that we thought we recognized almost a year later, and they did the same. It's kind of like one of those awkward thirty-fifth high school reunion moments when you fondly think you know a person but are still afraid to call them by name until a connection is made. Stopping outside Caleb's room to peer inside, a nurse broke the ice, and the blessings began to flow as five of his beautiful twenty-something nurses swarmed around him to reintroduce themselves. (I think Caleb wished he could've also remembered them too.)

As we stood soaking up the moment of Caleb making his own memories—and Sarah Kate sharing hers—a man slowly approached us, dressed in a Flight for Life jumpsuit. As his steps drew closer, Juri's very familiar face came into focus, but wearing a different uniform this time. Our excitement was uncontainable!

We were nearly speechless listening to Juri tell Caleb, "I would go by your room and pray for you at your Dad's request." Caleb was also excited to hear about Juri's music playing from his computer near Caleb's bed, knowing that he would've chosen the same genre had he been able to.

Word of Caleb's visit spread swiftly across the second floor's skeleton crew, and the chaplain soon joined the mini-gathering. She too had spent many hours in Caleb's room, praying during the night after all visitors had departed and we had told Caleb good night. She recalled a very particular moment when retreating to his room at three a.m., humbly admitting that it had been more about the tranquil peace she found there than it was about specifically praying for Caleb. With our love tanks full, we were abruptly reminded of where we were when the "code blue" sounded, and we watched the nurses scramble away to room 227.

The following day would include a return visit to see the day shift nurses and doctors, but one last event needed to take place at our familiar hotel dwelling before putting our tired bodies to bed. Pulling Sarah Kate close to his side, Caleb informed her that he had something for her. Handing Sarah a card, he thanked her for all she had done and sacrificed for him during the months since January.

In true Sarah Kate form, she *loved* the card—and *was not* expecting anything else. We laughed after quickly thinking about her also *loving* the box of walnuts she had unwrapped from Caleb and his cousins during a past Christmas, hoping to pull off a gift prank they'd seen on late-night television. It had backfired then, but tonight's gift didn't.

Caleb instructed her to close her eyes, hold out her hands, and guess what he'd just placed in them. Giggling but unable to guess, she opened her eyes and squealed with delight. I knew exactly how she felt, for I too had been blessed with unbelievable gifts in the past few hours. Though mine were not tangible, they were worth squealing over.

True to form, the *Jesus Calling* verse for this day spoke to our hearts: "You have made known to me the paths of life; you will fill me with joy in your presence" (Acts 2:28 NIV). We all slept well ... especially Sarah Kate. She cuddled her newfound treasure, rubbing Ella Bella against her skin as if remembering just how good her softness felt and just how much she'd missed the feeling. As the Waltons had done each week on TV when I was a child, the Jentsches exchanged good-nights as the lights went out: "Good night, Caleb. Good night, Kurt. Good night, Sarah Kate, and good night, Ella Bella." Each responded back in kind with a personal good-night to me, Sarah Kate doing so times two.

84

REINTRODUCTIONS CONTINUED

Our hotel breakfast buffet consumed, we drove a few blocks through leftover snow to the hospital, hoping for a morning as wonderful as the previous evening had been. With anticipation building again, the elevator on the trauma floor opened to a sweet young woman sitting at the concierge desk. Almost immediately recognizing us, she acted sincerely pleased to finally meet Caleb.

The number of TICU staff members on morning duty are as different from each other as night and day. As we turned the corner toward Caleb's room, our anxious steps passed many doctors and nurses focused on reviewing their morning briefs—just as we had remembered them doing every morning before rounds. Kurt's and my eyes locked onto Caleb's neurosurgeon and nurse, who were intently scrutinizing a computer as we finally stood silent some twenty feet away. I guess it's the feeling you have when someone is intently staring at you that made their synchronized double-take so priceless.

Bewildered, John and Becky stared over the monitor at the "diplomat" who had just arrived unannounced. Their blank stares soon turned to grins, and the joyful introductions were launched. Caleb hugged them both, and with a cracking voice they had never heard before, profoundly thanked them. A buzz began spreading on the second floor, which went viral, one nurse texting another, "I think Caleb is here!," as others began to warmly greet and welcome us back. And if that weren't enough amidst all the good chaos, the harpist was maneuvering through the hallway toward us, rolling her chair and harp. We once more poured into Caleb yet another experience from the hospital and, bless his heart, it had to feel like drinking unwrapped gifts from a fire hose. The harpist joyfully played the familiar renditions for us one more time, even being so kind as to let Sarah Kate strum the instrument's long strings.

While the music was once again a beautiful gift for my ears, my eyes fixated on an attendee gesturing over Caleb's arrival to a uniformed Flight for Life nurse standing nearby. Obviously being asked if he could find those who had transported Caleb to St. Anthony, his smile had already announced to me that he was one of the three, and knew who else to call to join the celebration. It was a good thing we had phones that acted like cameras, because the number of "flashcubes" required back in my day would have been costly.

Dave and Rich stood on either side of Caleb, and we captured this moment with arms around each other, which was so different from January 2012. Not only did they willingly agree to join in our photo op, but they escorted us upstairs to find the only doctor we had yet to see.

Dr. Yarnell had daily served Caleb and Kurt well and was still on staff at St. Anthony Hospital. He was by far the most seasoned neurologist on Caleb's team by at least a generation, and he still carried a small black doctor's bag to prove it. He wasn't only enthused to see us, but also keenly inquisitive, as one would expect a concerned, post-primary physician to be, asking Caleb numerous questions about his time in recovery. He instructed our son to walk and then closely admired Caleb's controlled movements up and down the hallway. He inquired about Caleb's drop foot and the current medications that he was taking, and once again he encouraged us as he had done so well before Caleb and Kurt had left in January. No handshakes were prescribed today, because only hugs had been totally anticipated.

Beyond our plans and expectations, we were given a private tour of Flight for Life's Control Center and then led to the helipad and shown a helicopter similar to the one that Caleb had been carried in. Gazing inside this piece of impressive machinery designed to help save lives by saving time, Rich vividly recalled that January afternoon when KSP's dispatcher had requested immediate help for a young male skier who had collided headfirst into a tree. Rich, David, and the pilot were already airborne and in standby over another emergency when Control Center relayed the urgent call for Caleb.

Hovering over a nearby mountain only five minutes from Caleb's location, the crew had already gained twenty-seven minutes over a flight originating from St. Anthony. Normal ER protocols were circumvented on Flight for Life's approach back as well, as they requested that Caleb go straight to CAT scan, due to the fact that he was, in Dave's words, a "very sick" patient. God saved those cumulative minutes for a purpose, and we continue to pray to see His plan revealed in Caleb's life today.

We moved through strategic areas of the hospital we had never seen before, retracing hastened steps that had taken Caleb directly from the helicopter to C-scan, and finally into surgery. It was a somber tour, mixed with a spirit of thankfulness. On a lighter observation, Sarah Kate was able to see some of her favorites back on the first floor, and just as she'd bonded with the trauma nurses, those in the cafeteria had come to know her well also. She was so proud to introduce her brother to the cashier who had worn a "Pray for Caleb" bracelet during the twenty-six days we were there.

We ate lunch in the cafeteria as a family and then dropped the guys off at the hotel. They chose to rest while Sarah and I made a Target run for snow pants. You just can't make a seven-year-old from Texas rest when she's in Colorado with snow on the ground. After returning from a successful shopping trip, and with the guys both refreshed, Sarah constructed a mini-snowman on the hotel patio table for all the guests to see.

Everyone agreed that it was definitely great to be seven.

CELEBRATION OF SERVING

The hospital's large dining room area also played host at another small table as we began setting up for an evening to see a few of Denver's special people. Reuniting never felt so good, with our "Texas girl," Kristen, now living in Colorado Springs; Aggie moms wearing their maroon and white who were always available when needed; Sara from the Denver A&M club, who had provided us with her car for numerous weeks; friends we made while in the waiting room who prayed faithfully for Caleb; Cole, Caleb's Bible study leader and friend at the BSM the previous year, and our Starbuck's connection; and the Smiths and family, who had come within an hour of Caleb's injury and continued to bless us immensely throughout the month that we were there.

It was so joyous to be gathered in that small area and sharing memories with one another, especially while watching Caleb being actively engaged in hearing about them. Though there were mostly smiles and hugs leading their introductions and conversations, it was the overly contagious tears of Susanna that I couldn't contain when she and Juri walked into the room. She too had chosen a career change, from trauma ICU nursing to the

Flight for Life team, largely influenced by Caleb and Flight for Life's efforts. She had been his first nurse during those critical hours when he'd arrived at St. Anthony and his life had depended on her. Other guests were able to slip away from their duties upstairs throughout the evening and take part in the "celebration of serving." It was a small thank-you from us to those who had wholeheartedly served us well in January.

Two nicely dressed individuals, appearing to be deep in a business dinner, hadn't gone unnoticed by Kurt and me while unloading before the celebratory evening began. They both wore badges representing St. Anthony, and apparently Kurt's Flight for Life jacket hadn't gone unobserved during their time together either. They politely stopped by our table and introduced themselves on their way out, being very much interested about our preparations for the evening. Understanding better their connection and influence with the hospital and its foundation, we were truly humbled to introduce Caleb and tell them that their diligent work did make a difference.

It's sometimes difficult not to lose sight of the trees for the forest—until one purposefully takes time to see an individual's name brought to life from paper. What a wonderfully divine opportunity it was to share Caleb's story and hear more about their work for the hospital. We had no inkling that we'd meet up again at another time, but for today this day was more than enough.

As this evening closed with many hugs and good-byes, no scripture shared our feelings better than Psalm 23:5 (NIV): "…You anoint my head with oil; my cup overflows."

86

PATROLS IN TRAINING

The ground was still covered with the early October snow, and the ice that was forming glistened as the sun shone upon it. The temperature was a mild thirty-five degrees, but it felt much warmer than a thirty-five-degree day does in Texas. We left our comfortable hotel in Denver to arrive at our beautiful abode overlooking a pond (complete with brown trout for Kurt) right outside Breckenridge, Colorado. Kurt's work associate, and friend, had offered us his condo nestled at the foot of a mountain area for our return visit, and we had readily accepted. We could have stayed nestled up for days ourselves, but tomorrow's agenda wouldn't allow for any delays.

Our drive led us to the sprawling Keystone Resort area, and silence enveloped our now thankful hearts to return to where our journey had begun for an event that was about to unfold. We parked in the lot across the road from the conference center and made our walk carefully across the season's first patches of ice to be met by Tracy once again. It was our first time to see her since that Thursday afternoon when she and Sarah Kate connected over a phone app, and she seemed to be as nervous and excited for the reunion as we were.

We formally introduced Caleb and loved on each other for several minutes. Tracy then escorted us to the main auditorium where one hundred and fifty ski patrol members had gathered from area resorts for three days to open the preseason ski patrol refresher. Eyes turned toward the door, and men and women rose to their feet with cheers and applause as Caleb was the first to enter. It was certainly unexpected, and it forced us all to tears, something we would come to expect for the rest of this day.

Craig moved swiftly from the podium to our family's side, emotionally welcoming us back before making the formal introductions. He was still leading Keystone Ski Patrol a season later, and he invited the men and women involved in Caleb's rescue to come forward as Caleb was being introduced. We too were now standing and applauding Caleb's first caregivers, and our applause shouted, "Thank you, thank you, many times thank you."

The event's main speaker was officially recognized, and Dr. Hudson began to implicitly explain the criticalness of KSP's role and response time in the life of an injured person before he ever had the opportunity to personally touch one in Denver's trauma ICU. He engaged this audience of seasoned veterans and first-season learners by presenting three different head trauma scenarios, and then asking how they would have responded to medically manage each one on the mountain. My heart beat faster when he described his final example as a twenty-one-year-old male. My eyes welled up with tears, ready to spill out.

As with the previous two individuals, Dr. Hudson revealed an image of this young man's brain shortly after arriving at the hospital. The surgeon explained that the collection of a large pool of blood and fluid between his skull and right front temporal lobe had been created by an initial impact, including the midline shift of his brain, and a deeper, severely bruised brain stem. White patches of sheared (torn) nerve axons could be seen across a herniated brain that had been violently thrown back and forth inside his skull after being abruptly stopped.

Dr. H went into greater detail than on the previous examples, explaining that KSP would have outwardly observed the severity of the injury by the male's right pupil, which had been blown by intracranial pressure. Paramedics would have initially scored him at a (GCS) level 3 before watching his body begin to posture in the rigid extension of his arms and legs pointed downward, and his head arching backward: the body's revelation that death was imminent.

Dr. Hudson paused and looked at a room that was intensely focused on him and eerily quiet. Arriving upon the scene of a skier with an injury as severe as this one, ski patrol would have known exactly what to do. Several veterans broke the silence, confidently shouting, "Try to control the swelling ... and get him off the mountain as quickly as possible!"

The presentation ended with Dr. Hudson showing a final CAT scan of his injured patient after surgically replacing his bone flap a mere three weeks later. Adhering to privacy policies, he didn't reveal the identity of the C-scan patient but closed by saying, "The bone flap was replaced, and Humpty Dumpty was put back together again." He asked Caleb to stand and then euphorically reintroduced him to Keystone Ski Patrol as Humpty Dumpty. Our applause was now directed toward Dr. Hudson and his wife.

Once again our thanks were not enough, but they were all we had to give.

Caleb was back in front of the large group, and those who had aided in his mountain rescue were invited to join him again. He was able to address them personally, and he did so with much emotion. He had the opportunity to share his faith and his blessing in knowing the realness of God when sometimes you doubt. He shared a verse from the song "Never Once," which summed up his belief that God had never once left us alone. He, with assurance, shared Nahum 1:7: "The LORD is good, a refuge in times of trouble. He cares for those who trust Him." He blew off extended handshakes from his incredible rescue team and went directly to big hugs and thank-yous.

As Caleb presented his closing thoughts before one hundred and fifty KSP members (which, if you think about it, would've been quite incredible *without* having a brain injury), the screen saver from Dr. Hudson's computer unknowingly began scrolling on the white board behind him. It was St. Anthony Hospital's mission statement, which read, "We extend the healing ministry of Christ by caring for those who are ill and by nurturing the health of people who are in our communities."

Caleb ended by asking Sarah Kate to stand with him at the front, sweetly thanking his sister for sacrificing her time during his healing. The hugs and handshakes from patrollers seemed endless, along with their, "Thank-you for coming back. We just don't get to see these outcomes once people leave the mountain."

We could honestly say, "The thanks are ours to give. Thank *you!*"

87

THE NORTH PEAK

When the morning's jubilation ended, we loaded into Craig's Texas-sized truck and rode up a sunlit mountain on a route we had never traveled before. The only way that we'd ever been up any of Keystone's three mountains was by way of chair lift or gondola, and it was a much longer ride than I anticipated, having to slowly traverse numerous switchbacks to climb the steep terrain. This road was the same service road that Caleb would have been brought down had the pilot decided not to land on the mountain that afternoon. We quickly concluded that this day most likely would've been one of sadness instead of celebration had Caleb's exit strategy off the mountain been different.

As our slow ascent continued, Craig paused his truck midway up to point out Flight for Life's landing spot after skiers were moved away from the base of the steep blue run Caleb had been skiing down. Though I couldn't picture or hear the helicopter, I imagined that it had been very loud, and the activity surrounding it very intense in the seriousness of the moment. Our road now quasi-paralleling the ski run, we traveled around several sharper turns before coming to a stop—almost directly across from the spot where KSP had first touched Caleb.

We unloaded from the truck into the freshly fallen snow, gathering our footing before we leaned into the mountain to cross the ski run. We were finally here, barely fifty yards directly up and over a steep incline where Caleb and Kyle had zigged and not zagged, accidentally crossing skis, with Caleb going headfirst into a tree.

Trying to reconcile what we'd always known with the cluster of tightly knitted trees coming into view, our eyes seemed to immediately settle on a large living one lying on its side in their midst. Red flagging had been purposefully tied around one of its protruding limbs, which had been exposed the season before due to a record minimal snowfall. The only sounds we heard in those next moments, which were few, were the sounds our deep breaths made from the mix of altitude and those that nature offered. We couldn't hear them, but our pounding hearts were racing.

Looking at this area, the possibilities of what had happened here on that January day of fun were hard to imagine, let alone try to communicate. Caleb showed much emotion as the videographer recorded his response to how he felt at the moment. Cabe couldn't come up with an answer to his question, because he wasn't really sure how he felt. He did find the ability within to express his gratitude for being able to come back to the site of his injury, which he had no memory of. He was allowed to take a few broken branches and cones from around the tree, and he gave thanks in prayer for his life and for those who had helped sustain it.

The trip back down to the base of the first mountain near the resort seemed equally long and was mostly without words. Caleb got to see and remember the gondola he and his friends had ridden up for many ski runs during previous years, and then he heard about the prayers painfully spoken during his absence on their last trip down. We shared Paul's words as he'd escorted the group of friends down the mountain, and how he had described the large cross slowly appearing as a finger had dragged against the fogged window. Paul had testified not only to praying for Caleb daily, but also to praying for his friends who had been affected by the circumstances of that day. Caleb was reminded of many, many events from that January afternoon, which he couldn't remember on his own.

At the end of this evening, we were all reminded to bless the Lord and forget not His benefits—and they were many. We had completed what we had come to Colorado for, and we would return to Texas to continue life as we now knew it.

88

WE WENT, WE SAW, WE RESTED

There were many benefits of our trip to Colorado, and what we had seen was beneficial to Caleb.

Returning to therapy the next week, he had a new perspective, knowing a little more about where he'd been in relation to where he was now. We all felt like we had been to the mountaintop and were rested and revived upon returning to our valley in Texas. It only took a few days until Kurt and I both hit what we call a wall. As always, we were quickly reminded of how we felt by Sarah Kate's favorite inquiring joke: "What did the fish say when it swam into the wall? *Dam!*"

Neither of us felt like we possessed the energy to encourage the other, and agreed with each other's diagnosis of emotional exhaustion. Fortunately, timely encouragement came through Sarah Young's devotional for this specific day: "Your weakness does not repel Me. On the contrary, it attracts My Power, which is always available to flow into a yielded heart. Do not condemn yourself for your constant need of help … Yielding yourself to My will is ultimately an act of trust. In quietness and trust is your strength."

The accompanying verse for my journal entry was: "Gracious is the LORD, and righteous; Yes, our God *is* merciful. The LORD preserves the simple; I was brought low, and He saved me. Return to your rest, O my soul, For the LORD has dealt bountifully with you." (Psalm 116:5–7 NKJV)

Rest, we have found, does not necessarily come from sitting in a chair for over an hour, or even from having the circumstances causing the angst removed. Rest will come from trusting the One in control and remembering that through any experience, He has been good to you. We sought to rest.

ANOTHER TIME CHANGE

You know you are on a longer-than-usual journey when the time to change your clock comes once again. We gratefully reset our clocks to regain the hour, which honestly Kurt and I hadn't mind losing on March 11th. No doubt, it had been one of our toughest days. The change in seasons allowed us to reflect back to the spring and truly value *all* of our time together as a family and to see the healing that God had brought into Caleb's life. Caleb was much more interested these days in his journey and recovery since our return from Colorado, and he especially enjoyed hearing about the more comical moments over the serious ones.

Caleb's energy level was increasing, and his medicine regimen was decreasing. It was our prayer that he'd maintain a higher energy level as medicines were withdrawn slowly, and he did. With the change in medications, a change in diet for Caleb (and for us) was also in the making.

Our oldest son, Eric, came home to spend some time helping us all out. His joy of cooking, and his knowledge of nutrition went hand in hand with the benefits and consequences of eating habits. Caleb too agreed that he needed to start a healthier plan. Eric is also extremely talented in all facets of artistic design, and helped Caleb fashion into a cross the few small limbs retrieved from Colorado. His opus included ideas suggested by Caleb and Kurt, and it displayed twelve small staples removed from Caleb's head and a torn piece of the bandana that had been cut away from around his neck. Caleb loved the finished work. The blessing came when he was allowed to present it to Kyle on the night of his baptism at their home church in College Station.

Eric's arrival in Victoria was also good timing, because Kurt's work during the last quarter of each year becomes exceedingly busier. Eric would help transport Caleb or Sarah wherever I deemed necessary, and he filled in the gaps at home when I was running the roads. Our weekly trip to Houston was extended this week by a day and included a follow-up visit to the eye doctor and Dr. Cassidy, an overnight stay at the Wedgeworths' house, and a brain-training session.

We waved at Kurt on the drive back to Victoria as he headed toward Houston for business. It truly felt like we were burning up the roads, but we still looked forward to our upcoming travels a week later and a wee bit further northwest—this time back to Wimberley. A week off for rest, starting a few days before Thanksgiving, sounded like just what the doctor ordered.

We even added a wedding celebration into our roadwork. And I wouldn't have known the groom who invited us, were it not for our time in Colorado. Cole was getting married, and it was our sincere treat to be part of his celebration. The bonus wasn't only the privilege of meeting his beautiful bride, but also his parents and extended family. Cole and Caleb's best friend Kyle are brothers, so this family gathering was a double blessing for me. It was evident why these young men were such ambassadors for Christ and His kingdom work. They had been taught well.

The venue was beautifully decorated and the perfect setting to also enjoy reuniting with Caleb's friends. Within an hour of the reception, Caleb had a look of distress on his face and was ready to leave. He expressed once again how difficult it was to be with his friends and then realize that life had truly gone on without him—and fearing that there wouldn't be a place for him once he returned. He listened to conversations he couldn't relate to and heard stories of fun times that he hadn't been able to be part of.

Fortunately, Joel related well to Caleb's feelings, assuring him that many students who went on mission trips for a semester felt the same way when they returned—reassuring words for me to hear from the BSM director—but Caleb didn't receive them fully as truth for lack of the connection. I was a little frustrated with Caleb because I knew none of this was an intentional act to leave him out. I insisted we stay until the cakes were cut, since Sarah Kate loves weddings so much.

On the trip back to Georgetown to spend the night with Mimi, our visit was revealing. Caleb explained that the nature of the conversations with his friends were mostly questions about his therapies and how they were going. It wasn't what Caleb wanted to talk about, since it really wasn't what he wanted to be doing in the first place. He wanted to be where they were. I truly empathized with him, and he thanked me for understanding and not instructing. It appeared Caleb was not being self-centered but self-aware, and in the background, that was something to be thankful for.

GAINING INDEPENDENCE

The next week in Wimberley provided creative opportunities for therapy sessions. Besides routine daily brain-training exercises, Caleb opted for physical therapy at Sea World, which required more than a great amount of walking. He navigated the climbing nets with Sarah and his nousin Emery, while I stood below watching him as deliberately as the mother next to me watched her toddler—ready to catch him should he fall.

We caught the last indoor show of the evening to end a wonderful day with a timely tribute to Shamu and the killer whale family. The extravaganza, titled "Miracles," was complete with testimonies playing on big screens throughout the filled stadium as the audience sang along to Christmas carols! Had it not been so rude or gotten us kicked out, I surely might have started jumping wildly up and down while pointing at Caleb and shouting, "Hey! Hey! Look over here! I am sitting with a miracle!" But calm prevailed within me, and I chose to simply sing out with our "miracle" and those surrounding me, "Let heaven and nature sing," knowing that God's *timing* is always perfect.

I could've sung the song again the following day atop Old Baldy. Caleb wanted to walk the 223 steps nonstop to the summit, and I stopped to catch a breather and to photograph a plaque halfway up that displayed the words "Come, let us go up to the Mountain of the Lord." When my aching, weary legs did make it to the top, I once again enjoyed a view of the Wimberley valley, which I have enjoyed for years. The scenic overlook showed growth in the valley, and organically, things most definitely hadn't stayed the same. After eleven months of what had mostly felt like an uphill climb, it was a great reminder that sometimes we have to be willing to work to reach the top before seeing God's panorama of what He has given us. It gave me a perspective different from the one at the foot of the hill. It was wonderful to stand at the top of this hill by Caleb's side.

As we celebrated Thanksgiving dinner with family in Mason, Texas, we gave many thanks for all of life's blessings. Kurt and I added to the thanks in our hearts as we celebrated life with Eric, Caleb, and Sarah Kate. Thank you, God, for our family. The week of Thanksgiving came to a close, and it was full steam ahead when we all hit the pavement in Victoria—back to therapies, work, school, and decorating for a new season.

Eric put Christmas lights on the house, and the artificial tree that had been up since last Christmas was moved from an unseen corner of a room to a corner now in view from two. The lights plugged into an outlet made it officially the "Christmas" tree again, and not just a tree with a hanging sign identifying the season. Caleb was preparing for a new season in his life, one that would offer him independence as he moved closer to the life he'd known before being hurt.

One of Caleb's northern-most steps toward independence was being able to share his journey with our church family during a Sunday morning worship service. Seated on stools in front of the congregation, Pastor Tim introduced Caleb and then asked a few leading questions to help set the stage for those who may not have known Caleb and HIStory. Caleb's answers were thought through and spot-on for all in attendance who had already walked our steps with us since January. He even jokingly referred to "slamming his head" into a tree, which the audience fittingly responded to with laughter—unless you happened to be his mother. Those words alone stirred fear in my being, and they make my stomach hurt today.

The interview led into a brief video showing Caleb the day after his January injury through that Sunday morning, December 2, 2012. Caleb had prepared it himself, and it was his testimony of thanks to all who had prayed and helped him through this journey. It was a testimony of Caleb's life verse, Nahum 1:7. And it was a testimony of God's faithfulness as a picture from his college freshman year stood frozen on the big screen with his hands raised toward a beautiful lakeside sunset.

The chorus to "10,000 Reasons" echoed: "Let me be singing when the evening comes … Bless the Lord, oh my soul." Appropriately, the final words sat on the screen in white font against a black background and resonated: "Now to him who is able to do immeasurably more than all we ask or imagine, according to his power that is at work within us, to him be glory in the church and in Christ Jesus throughout all generations, for ever and ever! Amen" (Ephesians 3:20–21 NIV).

I'm not sure about all the other eyes in His house, but I do know mine and those close around me were brimmed to overflowing, each tear in awe and thanks to God for His immeasurable "more."

91

ONE MONTH TO RELEASE

Release was what we had continually prayed for during the past eleven months, but it now caused fear to rise within.

We had prayed for Caleb to be released from St. Anthony Hospital, and he had been. We had prayed for Caleb to be released from TIRR Memorial Hermann, and he was. We had longingly prayed for Caleb to be released from Touchstone to come home, and he was. There were other releases that he had experienced also. He'd been released from his wheelchair to walk, from his dream state to reality, and from taking particular medications. He'd been released to take weekend excursions with friends, and released from brain training after completing it. And now he would soon be released from outpatient therapy.

We knew it was *now* our moment to decide whether to personally release Caleb from *our* care to go back to school and independent living—or not. This was what we had prayed for all along, but we weren't sure if he was completely ready. To be honest, he probably wasn't ready the first time we released him to leave home and go to A&M as a freshman. The truth of the matter here was that our release was more to God than to anything else, and that still, small voice continued to speak the same words we had heard many times over: "Trust Me."

We were going full circle to the day when I'd read those words prior to Caleb's "slamming into a tree."

WRINGING IN 2013

It was our first time ever to celebrate New Year's Eve in College Station. This college town, void of most of its students, was probably less active on New Year's Eve than on most Thursday nights when school is in session. We came in two cars to move Caleb back into the house on Merry Oaks Dr., where he had lived before taking an injury time-out.

Caleb was insistent about moving back upstairs into the room he had stayed in during the fall of 2011. I was hesitant and repeatedly objected because of the lack of a handrail and an open wall near the bottom of the steps, but my objections were continually overruled. Later in the semester, Caleb admitted that he might have preferred a downstairs bedroom, but it had nothing to do with my handrail argument. He had discovered that he often needed to go back upstairs several times a day because of something he'd forgotten. Since climbing the stairs required more physical exertion than it had last year, frustration now accompanied his steps when making the extra trips. The additional therapy was counted as a blessing in the long run to help stimulate his right foot and toes.

As if to prove my climacophobia wrong, Caleb carried eight bins of his belongings upstairs from the garage area where they'd been housed for the last twelve months. Unpacking began, and it was all finished before Kurt, Sarah Kate, and Jazzy arrived. They would be coming behind us from Victoria because of car issues, with Kurt *patiently* waiting for the needed repairs to be completed. I could only imagine his thoughts after picking up the car, loading in all of Caleb's belongings from home, and turning the key— only to hear, click … click … click.

It appeared the distractions were mounting, and after Kurt jumped the battery and drove three hours nonstop in the misting rain with a seven-year-old and the dog, he was worn out. I'd love to tell you I greeted him in College Station with empathy and love, but I too was worn out, and we collided. After exchanging unkind words, we confessed that God is good and we are not. The unseen stresses were bubbling through, and we had to choose to release them to God.

Caleb trusted that the New Year would arrive in College Station after he watched the East Coast celebrations and then went upstairs to bed. We gave it our best effort to let Sarah stay up until midnight, said "Happy New Year," and then turned out the lights at 12:05 a.m. The year 2012 was now in the record books, and 2013 would soon begin to reveal itself.

Before leaving College Station, we met on campus with Caleb's first assigned disability counselor, as his first semester back in college was now just a few short weeks away. We believed the provisions being made to help him succeed would be beneficial, and we thank Texas A&M University for offering one of the best programs in the country.

Caleb's calendar was synced with his counselor's to meet once a week after the semester start, and Caleb didn't plan to miss a single appointment. Besides being very compassionate and helpful, Sarah was young and beautiful, and we were confident she'd do her best to help Caleb throughout the semester … and she did.

93

VICTORY DAY

We didn't need a GPS to direct us from College Station to Wimberley where a small team of Caleb's friends joined us a few days later. The rest were traveling to Dallas for the Cotton Bowl and would send their love out over the radio through the play-by-play announcer, who also gave a shout-out to Caleb on his injury anniversary. He too wished him the very best in his upcoming return to College Station.

Our great room was loud and proud as mesmerized eyes watched Johnny Football elude defenders and lead the Aggies to outscore their opponent for the win. Manziel often appearing to be tackled and down—only to emerge for a touchdown—brought about roars from amazed and excited fans. I too thought, *Wow, how did he do that?*

Those words leaving my lips reminded me of the many times Caleb had appeared to be defeated over the last twelve months, only to emerge from under whatever was trying to hold him down. Johnny was always honest enough to give credit to his team and coaches following the game, recognizing that he couldn't have accomplished the victory alone. We too would have the opportunity to thank those who were part of the team for Caleb and had helped him in the victories evident so far. It was summed up best on a gift Caleb received that same evening, a plaque that read, "I can do all things through Christ who strengthens me."

We gave thanks to God at the top of "Old Baldy" after climbing the multiple steps one more time. Pastor Tim reminded Caleb and his Aggie friends of God's words to Moses, and His promise that Moses would see His accomplishments upon returning to the mountain where they had first met. For Moses these were reassuring words of things he hoped God would bring about, and the foundation that He would use for things yet to come.

This kind of faith was never intended to help us travel *around* mountains. It was always His plan to help us *experience* them as Kurt and I remembered the pain from exactly one year before, actually feeling the weight of our heartaches when recalling the events of that day. To add to the heaviness of our hearts, Caleb was tired and went to sleep, crying, "Couldn't there have been another way?"

Rest served him well overnight, and he updated the CaringBridge site the next morning, thanking all who had followed and supported him through their prayers and actions during the course of the past year. He ended the post, saying, "This may be weird to hear, but I am okay with what has happened, and I am kinda glad that it did ... But really take some time to dwell on what this means, as I am planning to do every night before I lay down in bed. The LORD is good, a refuge in times of trouble.

He cares for those who love him, who have been called according to his purpose."

It had always been our intent to stop the updates on January 6 after a full year of posting, but many people asked to be kept informed of Caleb's school progress as they continued to pray for him. We thank CaringBridge for affording us the opportunity to do so.

We drove Caleb back to College Station on my birthday to help him with last-minute preparations before the semester started. He considered not being able to drive one of his greatest hardships, and it proved to be most difficult at times. I was thankful he had been restricted from driving, because it was one less concern I might *choose* to worry about.

Cabe texted me upon our return to the hotel, saying he was sorry about not fulfilling last year's birthday wish when I had hoped he would open his eyes. He had definitely looked into my eyes today, and I had assured him it was all okay.

His second text contained the words we had repeated at bedtime for most of his life: "I love you to heaven and back!" What a wonderful birthday gift I had received!

94

LEFT BEHIND

We left Caleb in good hands—God's hands—ready for a fresh start in a new season of life. He was signed up for three spring semester classes totaling seven hours, one hour being bowling. I didn't dare tell him of my own college bowling class struggles where more pins stood than fell. Honestly, I had very little concern at this point whether his pins did either. I was solely thankful Caleb was able to stand after his fall.

I listed many prayer requests for those who continued to pray for Caleb: that he would find favor with professors and classmates; that he would bless professors, classmates, friends, and family; that his working memory would continue to heal and serve him well; that he would continue to show patience and take initiative; that he would not feel like a burden to others when asking for rides; that he would be able to maneuver the large campus; that his executive planning would increase and good time management would be evident; that he would return to his church and Bible study groups…; and that *our own faith and trust* would *increase* as he was outside of our watchful eye.

A message was so directed to me from Mark Batterson's book, *Draw the Circle*, on the day we left Caleb. He reminded me that God keeps the earth rotating in the universe while I sleep at night, and the sun still rising after I've had a full night's sleep. I honestly don't know how we were able to drive out of the College Station city limits without crying, except that we were reminded of who is really in control. We were not leaving Caleb in the hands of Texas A&M, his professors, his friends, or his church. We were entrusting him to God, the One who had healed him to the point of our having a *choice* about where he would be this spring of 2013. I was glad for confidence on this day, for it would be shaken in days ahead.

When we drove away Sunday afternoon, our strength from God was extended through the community of people who love Caleb. He attended church with his church family during the evening and returned home to roommates who had his best interest at heart. Besides having fabulous friends, he had cousins there who'd do anything for him. With everyone from the supportive village surrounding him, it was a hard conversation to have with Caleb when he called and said, "I feel left out."

We couldn't discount his feelings; we could only try to help him determine the reality of why he felt that way. The truth was, he'd been left out for much of the last year by no one's choice, but by the circumstances of his injury. To fit back in would take time, adjustment, and patience on his part. Since this was only Monday and the first day back in classes, we questioned our decision to send him back so soon. We suggested changing his thoughts, resting, and waiting on the newness of the next morning. We would repeat this same advice to ourselves after we hung up the phone.

The next morning was refreshing for Caleb after spending time in the Word with his roommate. He then went on to his bowling class where he met his professor for the first time and asked him about his faith. Lunch at the student center with friends followed, and that was when the second distress call came in. It seemed his friends had stepped away to converse with others, and an overwhelming feeling of being left alone consumed Caleb.

I was in the grocery store when his text pinged me: *"Things are not going well. Can you come get me? I want to talk to you face-to-face. Mom, it's a roller coaster ride!"* Then he expressed how much he hated it. If my broom could fly, I would've zoomed over College Station, swooped him up, and brought him back to the nest. Instead I texted him back: "I can't come today, but I will come."

He was not letting up, and his next message asked, *"Can Dad come today?"* I responded by saying that I'd call Dad and ask, but he wasn't satisfied with my answer and said he'd call Dad himself! My fingers couldn't type fast enough to relay a message to Kurt before he answered Caleb's anxious call requesting a ride home from College Station *today!* Their abbreviated conversation was divinely interrupted by his friend's return and Caleb telling Kurt, "Hey, I will call you back."

That was on Tuesday afternoon, and the return call back was not until Wednesday evening. Cabe sent some texts in the interim, saying he was having dinner with friends, had been to Breakaway Ministries on campus, was meeting with the BSM director, and had spent time in prayer with his roommates before going to bed.

We could really relate to Caleb's analogy of a roller coaster, because it felt like Kurt and I were in the front car—*holding on with all our strength*! Once again the Bible highlighted a story we could link to our circumstances and find strength in. The verses instructed one to keep his eyes on the Master and not the waves crashing all around him. At the moment Caleb had said, "Come get me," I knew the sinking feeling Peter had felt while on the water. The waves of despair crashed upon me and I desperately cried out for help. Immediately, a few friends began to pray. Things changed. Kurt and I prayed wholeheartedly for wisdom, and we were changed. It occurred to me when Caleb had earlier asked his professor about his faith, the spiritual warfare increased, and Caleb was being attacked with "flaming arrows" of doubt and fear.

We know from the Word of God that He does not give us a spirit of fear, but of power, love, and a sound mind. We were thankful for those who continued in the battle with us for "things" to change, and we were moved to stand on solid ground. Joshua 1:9 (CSB) completed our posting for this day by asking for prayers: "Haven't I commanded you: be strong and courageous? Do not be afraid or discouraged, for the LORD your God is with you wherever you go."

THE PUBLIC AIRWAVES

Caleb would call or text over the next few weeks with questions and concerns but thankfully wasn't in a crisis mode. Most of his questions were asking for recipes to take to a social event on his calendar, and we gladly obliged. He struggled with asking others for a ride to places and was constantly asking us when his day would come to drive again. We relayed the question again to his doctor, and we knew Caleb would not be pleased with his answer. Dr. Cassidy continued to play the bad guy and wasn't willing to release Caleb back to the roads just quite yet.

We really didn't understand why asking for a ride to and from an event posed such difficulty for Caleb. He explained that it had more to do with the freedom to leave a function than actually asking to get there. He almost always found himself becoming tired before an event ended and wanted to return home, yet he didn't want to ask someone to leave before they were ready. We now understood Caleb's frustration level and his "thought-out" struggle to not impose his dependence upon others. His needle still continued to point north.

His seven-hour class load was already light for a college student, and it dropped to four hours after a few weeks into the semester. We wanted to make the best decision for Caleb's overall recovery and the larger picture of returning to school and managing a life of independence, not just for his education outcome. Caleb wasn't able to follow the computer instructions in his class at the speed it was moving, and time management was proving to be an ongoing battle.

In an effort to help, his professor gave him an option to make up a missed quiz by memorizing and reciting George Carlin's, "Seven Words You Can't Say on Radio or Television." Although this may be relevant information in a radio class where over four hundred thousand different words could've been chosen from, we decided this wasn't relevant in Caleb's healing (especially after learning that we'd already heard most of the words from recovering Touchstone residents who knew no better).

It just didn't seem this information was something that Caleb really needed to try to commit to memory, and it was confirmed in the form of a text from a friend, saying, "God is with us and God is for us ... that's all you need to know." We decided Caleb would be best served by focusing solely on bowling and his writing class.

96

WHO MOVED MY CHEESE?

We visited Caleb the following weekend and tried to help him deal better with the difficulties of life after a brain injury—organizationally. Attempting to help set up his tests for his online classes, it became apparent that we weren't capable. He needed to seek outside assistance.

The phone call from Caleb a few days later was an enlightening conversation when we heard that his professor had gone well beyond the normal requirements to help Caleb prepare for the best possible success. I was excited to hear that his humanities professor was practicing what she preached. We'd see evidence of the same best practices emerge from other meetings Caleb initiated with professors in various fields of study. These were acts we didn't expect.

After one particular afternoon meeting, Caleb also took the *initiative* (which Kurt continued to preach) to ride a shuttle bus home for the first time rather than calling someone to come and taxi him. Upon exiting the bus at the stop closest to his house, he wasn't exactly sure which direction to go. Surveying landmarks that looked familiar, he headed off in their direction, proudly navigating the long way home of at least a mile to Merry Oaks Drive. In light of his usual amount of physical exercise in any given day, today's effort was a lot at this point in his recovery. I was just thankful I was hearing about this happy ending from Kurt *after* Caleb reached home safe and sound, or I might've found myself radioing for another search and rescue mission.

There were also other times during the semester when I was definitely more panic-stricken than my son. He was ready to hit the send button to submit a two-page humanities paper, but after reading through the instructions one last time, I realized that his composition needed to be at least five pages long! Caleb's only response was, "Really?" And he determinedly began making the required additions. The cool thing was Caleb's ability to retain and connect a timeless story to his injury *from his own memory.* He had written subjectively concerning the book, *Who Moved My Cheese?*, personally identifying with the mouse character, Sniff, whose cheese had been moved and who now had new obstacles in place to get to it. Caleb had maneuvered well around his own new obstacles and received an A for the opportunity.

Caleb experienced many roadblocks daily and was forced to learn unaccustomed ways to successfully complete what had at one time been simple routine. Some school days were more challenging than others, and his written bowling test proved to be more difficult than writing his paper or physically bowling. After receiving his grade, his claim to success was, "I didn't make the lowest grade in the class, but I sure felt sorry for the one who scored lower than a kid with a brain injury.'" Fortunately, his bowling skills test made up for his lack of memory, and he ended up with a passing grade and another hour of credit.

Caleb may have had to drop his radio class, but he still covered the public airwaves. He and Kyle were interviewed by a local TV station, which aired on the nightly news in College Station. Both gave their accounts of Caleb's injury during his absence from school, and each then gave his testimony about Caleb's recovery—the evidence that God had received glory in so many circumstances throughout the last year.

God remained faithful to Caleb to show how He intended to use his injury for the good He promises in Romans 8:28. Caleb was thankful for the opportunity to share his story as he showed off his bowling skills for the TV camera, only twelve months after his injury.

97

GOOD TO GO!

Caleb continued to make gainful strides during his first semester back, achievements that weren't measured in other college students. He would be challenged to remember to take his medications, work to increase endurance, and negotiate everyday tasks that had required very little cognitive effort during semesters prior to his injury. These efforts were taxing on Caleb, both mentally and physically. He had to make good decisions on achieving sleep when most college students were prepping to go out and socialize. He was discouraged at times by the fact that he wasn't able to live the "normal" college life he had before. His discouragement was usually short-lived, and he regrouped to make wise choices after personally considering the outcomes. He didn't agree with all the choices made on his behalf, however—such as his inability to drive. But he cooperated nonetheless, patiently waiting for the end of the semester when he'd be allowed to test behind the wheel.

In preparation for this hallmark event, Dr. Cassidy ordered an EEG midsemester to assess Caleb's brain for any seizure activity that might further prolong his decision. The report after the sleep study was "good," so Dr. Cassidy again began tapering off another medication—and gave Caleb his blessing to try to drive.

"Good to go" was also the report at the end of the semester from his driving instructor. With his first semester complete and now on his transcript, Caleb managed an intense day of both classroom and driving assessment, which actually required him to drive defensively in Houston traffic on a *busy* IH 10 at four o'clock in the afternoon. It was a test for the most seasoned driver, and I'm thankful I wasn't informed of the course selection before Caleb pulled away from the parking lot.

Caleb showed his comedic side when he phoned Kurt after the test—having received his release to drive—as I drove us to our resting place for the night. "Hi, Dad. How are you doing?" he inquired. "Yes, sir, I'm doing great too, thanks ... Driving test? ... Yes, sir, I passed my test, and I'm able to drive ... Thanks, it was great ... Yes, sir, I drove with my instructor on Interstate 10 at four o'clock today ... No, really, Dad, I did ... But hey, Dad, they also wanted me to practice making a phone call and talking while I drive, so that's why I'm calling you."

Though unable to see Kurt's facial expression or hear his loss for words, I knew he must be wearing a look that expressed, "Oh, My Lord, please tell me this isn't so, God!" Caleb quickly relieved Kurt's induced palpitations. "Just kidding, Dad. Mom's driving."

Seeing Dr. Cassidy the following day, Caleb reported on the remainder of his semester since visiting last and then shared some exciting news. Not only had he regained his driver's permit; he would also finally be ordering his Aggie class ring after completing the four hours needed to introduce him into the Aggie network! He told Dr. Cassidy he'd be taking a break from course work over the summer months, and that he already had many plans inked in on his calendar (away from home).

It would be an especially challenging post-injury summer, because Caleb hadn't spent any summers at home since his junior year of high school, and there were no plans for this semester break to be any different. Caleb wouldn't see Dr. Cassidy again until after the end of summer—and would only then give him his itinerary details.

FIRST SUMMER AWAY FROM HOME

Caleb's first commitment was full days of counseling at a Christian camp with students striving to grow in their relationship with Christ. Much of Caleb's spiritual growth started as a youth during his weeks at Super Summer. Less than a month after completing his initial commitment, Caleb would then travel with high school students, co-joined with the iGo Global Ministries. This too would be new territory for Caleb geographically, but his familiarity with iGo's evangelism efforts was not, since he had served as an intern in recent summers while in high school and college. Not only would it be a challenging time for Caleb, both physically and mentally, but Kurt and I were once again challenged parentally to continue to let go.

It was especially hard to allow Caleb to drive solo 120 miles from Wimberley to Belton, Texas, up busy Interstate 35N on his first road excursion to stay a week at Super Summer. The whole family then escorted him to Dallas three weeks later to attend iGo Global's base camp, which was held the weekend before the group departed for Madrid, Spain. These packed forty-eight hours were spent preparing the kids (and their parents) both mentally and spiritually for the trip abroad. Being a mom, I stayed around for a night to volunteer with others in the created land of Igosia—and to be assured that Caleb was able to adjust.

God tested me early on in base camp to reveal exactly who I was placing my trust in. Within hours of arriving at the twenty-acre facility, I was summoned from the kitchen to an outside area around the cabins where Caleb was sitting on the sidewalk surrounded by his peers. En route to his and others' rooms to store their personal belongings, he had tumbled off the back of a golf cart while steadying himself on a piece of luggage engineered to roll. From all observations, Caleb was fine and would still participate as an adult chaperone with the students overseas.

I prayed that evening, "Dear, Lord, please help me to continue to place my trust in You, the One who gives peace. May the joy that You promise me come in the morning." I reread the CaringBridge entry for this exact date a year before, and my spirit was encouraged by the healing that had brought us to this point. My blog then had also requested prayers for Caleb's *joy* to return.

In the midst of this camp and these people on a mission he loves, Caleb's joy was captured through a video presentation showing the students' first twenty-four hours on the campground. Caleb's face flashed on the screen, and it was evident: his infectious smile and sparkling eyes *radiated* joy. I was unable to contain my own feelings and could only express through tears of joy what I was experiencing.

With the group session formally over, I got Caleb's attention long enough for him to tell me what cabin he was staying in so I could deliver an extra pillow for his first night. "I am in the cabin named Joy," he said. "Of course it is!" I replied laughingly. Caleb could in no way understand why his answer had brought me such pleasure—even before the morning came.

Caleb departed for Spain for ten days with fifteen high school students and four other adults, and did well for the most part. There were a few times when he felt defeated, and those moments were steered by fatigue and managed with rest. The fatigue followed him home in the form of jet lag, which required almost a full week to overcome. That was all the recovery time available, because another camp for incoming freshman at A&M was beginning the following week. He also had the small detail of moving into a different house before a new semester started. We were all in awe of how quickly time had passed since Caleb was home with us for the brief summer.

The fall of 2013 at A&M contained different challenges from his first semester back. Receiving what he had asked for, driving again required Caleb to navigate through College Station traffic, which can prove to be as crazy as Houston's. He was challenged by the arrangements of a new house and three new roommates who were all younger than he was, and a course load that increased from four to eleven hours. His biggest struggle was being a fifth-year senior and finding "his place" again in the midst of it all.

I'm sure I struggled more than Caleb did as I drove away from his new living quarters toward home. Sarah Kate said, "I am going to miss him," and I could barely choke out the words, "Me too."

I drove for the next two and a half hours, sobbing as silently as I could, my thoughts expressing the anger I felt with the present situation. The conflict within me raged, and I prayed that at the end of this battle my heart would be changed.

99

THE THREE R'S

It's an answer to your children's question, which you learn later in parenting that it is okay to give. Early on as parents, we thought we needed to know all the answers, even when we didn't. We finally became wise enough, or old enough, to honestly confess our lack of knowledge.

We had to tell Caleb, "We don't know," when he called home during the start of the fall semester to ask if his energy level was as good as it was going to get, or if his memory was as sharp as it was ever going to be. Although a conscious concern for Caleb, he was able to manage through the tough moments of a full semester, and we only saw him for twelve hours during the first six weeks. One weekend within that semester would be worth all the struggle, a milestone in Caleb's life and a moment he'd anticipated for many years.

As soon as we were on the road to College Station, I checked my phone's weather app to see if the hard rain we were driving through was being forecast for the remainder of the weekend. It was. The moisture wouldn't keep any of the thousands of Aggies away from Ring Day. It's the day marking completion of ninety college credit hours at the university, and a ring to identify you to the rest of the Aggie nation. For those supporting Caleb, this was an "exceedingly, abundantly more" day.

Arriving on campus an hour prior to Caleb's scheduled time to receive his ring, we all stood under pelted umbrellas, knowing that this was a time to rejoice and not feel rained on. Covert plans had already been underway and finagled late into the afternoon, complete with the twists and turns of an undercover movie in deciding who would present Caleb with his ring.

Cabe had previously asked his grandfather to do the honors, but thinking through the few remaining hours, he decided that his own dad should make the presentation. Met with 100 percent approval from Granddaddy, my daddy cried when telling me about Caleb's request weeks before. His tears turned to excitement minutes later when Kurt revealed a new change of plans developing behind closed doors. Through an exchange of text messages, Kurt confirmed that Dr. Loftin would be more than honored to formally give Caleb his ring. Caleb was expecting to surprise his dad—only to be surprised by his dad in return.

Cameras were clicking as Caleb hugged his dad, his granddaddy, and the President of Texas A&M University among the families and friends gathered to witness the thousands who received their rings. Pictures taken would be a remembrance for years to come, and Caleb walked away with new jewelry symbolizing his last step toward graduation. Caleb was so thankful.

Our celebration moved to a rented condo where we *all* gave thanks for the three Rs for this day. The *rain* reminded us just how powerless we were; we couldn't make it happen and couldn't make it stop. We could choose to rejoice in it or grumble about it. The *ring* reminded us of the blessing of life and God's decision for Caleb to live. On this day in 2013, Cabe received his class ring with a '13 embossed on it—in the 13th group of newly commissioned Aggies. The last *r* represented *relationships*. There were many represented in today's celebration, both present and afar. It was a time to stop and give thanks for all who had helped Caleb get to this day.

Caleb finished strong, adding ten more hours to his grand total. He established a great rapport with one of his professors, working hard not only to achieve a good grade, but more importantly, to build a relationship that they both treasured. He encouraged Caleb, providing opportunities for learning and success well beyond any written words in a textbook. This professor will go down in our history books as one of "the greatest of all times."

100

SPILLWAY

At the completion of the fall semester, an awaited trip back to Colorado was now ahead of our family. Our invitation to return came via a phone call from the same precious lady who had stopped by our table to meet us before our October "celebration of service." She informed us that she was on the hospital foundation's event planning committee and was spearheading this year's annual gala benefitting St. Anthony's new neuroscience wing.

Caleb's name was an already familiar one when suggested to the committee of physicians and board members to be one of two honorees. Their decision was unanimous. We were asked to come back for a fundraising gala in January where Caleb and Mindy would share their stories through a short film during the banquet. It was with great pleasure that we could now *sing* out a "yes" to this invitation.

Our initial phone interview took place from our home in November and consisted of a conference call between the film production team, a foundation member, and Kurt and me. As the creative writer began hearing Caleb's story for the first time, he abruptly interrupted to ask about personally interviewing Caleb as well. Our response was our reality: "We have no hesitation with your interviewing Caleb, but he does not—nor will he ever—personally remember his stay at St. Anthony. His four months bound by post-traumatic amnesia will prevent him from remembering any of his time spent recovering in Colorado and TIRR, and most of his time at Touchstone in Texas."

We loved being part of the hospital's vision to provide a new facility dedicated to carrying patients *and* their families through a continuum of care, minimizing the related stress that comes from moving families from one facility to the next. Our conference call lasted well over two hours, and many rabbits were chased in and out of holes, which only God could have orchestrated the answers to.

We also tried our best to verbally fill a big, blank canvas, which said, "While this story has much to do with Caleb and St. Anthony Hospital, God has always used this afternoon for the much larger purpose of "making Himself famous." We just hoped and prayed that our painting would begin to reveal who was truly in complete control over Caleb, and was already making a way for him on January 5, 2012. In an effort to help our discussion, Kurt forwarded both an *e-mail* sent by a trusted source from Keystone's Ski Patrol, and a *CaringBridge update* from January.

Several events combined to aid in Caleb's rapid transport from the mountaintop to the helipad atop St. Anthony Hospital. From the email we learned:

> The sweeps to clear the skiers on Spillway and Anticipation ski
> runs had just begun placing patrollers within seconds of Caleb's

location—meaning three trained patrollers arrived almost immediately after learning there was an injury on Spillway.

The paramedic working on January 5 was known to be one of the best and was on duty after misreading the schedule for that day.

The KSP supervisor in charge of snowmobiles, who was one of the most capable snowmobile drivers, was near the paramedic and able to rapidly transport him across a rather treacherous route to the location where Caleb was being treated and prepared for transport.

Refusing to accept no as an answer, the KSP dispatcher on duty convinced the Flight for Life dispatcher and pilot to land. The flight crew was already in an emergency standby assist mode over Mt. Evans, five minutes from Caleb's location, but the helicopter was not fitted with the appropriate skis to land on the mountain.

The patrollers were disheartened when hearing there were no flights at that time and a transport of about an hour down the mountain would be their only choice—until they observed a helicopter overhead coming their direction. Their spirits soared.

There had been many orchestrated hands and voices involved in transporting Caleb quickly and safely.

January's CaringBridge Update:

"We have learned in emergency medicine that the 'golden hour' refers to the time period, lasting anywhere from a few minutes to several hours, when prompt medical treatment may prevent death following a traumatic injury. For Caleb, the estimate was an hour and five minutes from the time Keystone Ski Patrol first got to Caleb on the mountain to when he was laid on the operating table at St. Anthony. 'Orchestrated' with Flight for Life's close proximity to Caleb, we later learned the timeline was reduced by the assistant neurosurgeon's decision to leave another case in OR and move Caleb quickly "through the ER admission channels" as his stats and arrival time aired over the hospital's loudspeakers.

"Jeff had worked trauma in Special Forces previously and knew time was critical to get Caleb into surgery quickly. Along with Jeff's wisdom was John's availability (a neurosurgeon who was not on call) and protection as he sped close to one hundred miles per hour down a six-lane, inner-city street to meet Caleb's arrival and perform a surgery, which he not only survived, but to repair a severely injured brain—something many of you had already been specifically praying for John to be able to do. A 'golden hour' chock-full of many details that came together from beginning to end in every sense of those words."

━━━━◆◆◆◆◆━━━━

The Integer production team began to grasp the timing of events and the many details God had already put in place on a ski run named Spillway. Everyone agreed on the phone that Kurt and I would provide most of the information on the front end of filming, while Caleb would testify to coming back to the place where the journey had begun. The most moving moment of our time with the team after returning to Colorado in December was just prior to filming, when Caleb requested to pray. All agreed and were moved emotionally.

"Did we get that on tape?" asked the producer. They had not, and Caleb was asked if he would pray again. He chuckled at the thought of praying for a taping, and agreed to close in prayer at the end.

101

ONWARD

We said our good-byes after two hours of filming and headed west back to the same familiar mountains of Colorado for a time of rest and more celebration. Sitting on the couch at the condo with my morning's coffee and Caleb, I could see the mountains outside and the snow falling gently upon them. A sip of coffee, and I opened my devotional to the bookmark for day 122 from Sarah Young's *Jesus Today*, and I *could not* believe what I was reading. "I am Good—a refuge in times of trouble, I care for those who trust in Me" (Nahum 1:7 NIV). The day's devotion went further with a written verse Caleb had been drawn to since last summer and throughout the semester: "Go and make disciples!" (Matthew 28:19–20 NIV). What a special moment, knowing it was no coincidence! Rather, it was a loving Father affirming His promises to us by preparing this devotion for me in advance of this day.

Our time spent in the mountains was so soothing and only heightened over dinner with the fellowship of Craig and his family. He too personally reflected on those initial hours during that sunny afternoon, and the emotions he had struggled with as a father. He and Caleb laid out future plans to ski on the mountains of Keystone together after he graduated from A&M—alongside a team of patrollers. I was able to agree in advance, knowing that Craig was already looking out for this mother and her fears.

The holiday break was soon over, and Caleb returned for his final spring semester on the campus of A&M and eleven scheduled hours. He faced what would probably be his greatest challenge of his college career in a Finance class. He called us on the night of the Super Bowl, discouraged at his inability to grasp the information required for his first test. When asked to read me a question, I stopped him midway through, thinking he was reading more than the question. "Mom, that still *is* the question!" I then knew that this was going to be an extremely difficult course, and he was going to need more help than we'd planned for him in advance.

Thankfully, the professor recognized Caleb's efforts in and outside of her classroom and was willing to provide for his needs. She helped him find success as Cabe's other professor had so willingly done the semester before. Cabe's hard work and commitment to all his classes was unquestionable only two years after he'd been severely brain injured. His determination was nowhere close to medical science expectations, let alone *any* medical expectations that he'd be back in college in the first place. Caleb continued to surprise and amaze Kurt and me with phone calls telling us about his time spent studying, additional meetings outside scheduled class time with his teacher assistants, and his plans to ultimately succeed.

Everyone was moving onward in the "new normal," and it was looking mighty good to us.

102

THE GALA

Two weeks into the 2014 spring semester, we made our final trip back to Colorado for the gala in Denver, arriving to unusually warmer temperatures than those we'd experienced when departing from Austin, Texas. The Denver Marriott accommodated the evening's grand event as well as our room, and we checked in early enough to witness a ballroom being transformed into a bright and beautiful venue awaiting over seven hundred attendees in black-tie attire.

Caleb looked outstanding in his rented tuxedo as he descended into a large room full of people already registered and milling about. We anxiously moved slowly through the silent auction room's three hundred displayed items to find his brother's painting, which Eric had specifically painted for the fundraiser. The four tall trees standing in a sunlit Colorado snow, and the one fallen in front of them, depicted our family. It brought us great pleasure to watch a silent bidding war develop between the hospital's director and the co-honoree for his beautiful rendition, knowing that Eric wished he could've been with us too.

We saw many unfamiliar and familiar faces as we walked throughout the room, and we were delighted to spot Integer's team among them. Kurt and I had previewed and approved their final production two weeks earlier, but Caleb chose to wait and watch it for the first time tonight. After exchanging laughter and hearing words of congratulation from those we knew and the many that we met during the social hour, we retreated to our assigned seats for the start of an even more incredible evening.

The dinner and conversation were filling as Caleb's and Mindy's stories became familiar to those seated around our table. It was our special honor to be seated with the co-honoree and her husband, for her story was both moving and inspiring. Their familiarity soon spread quickly beyond our table as the master of ceremonies approached the podium to announce the program's agenda and to introduce the evening's guests, including Caleb and Mindy.

Cued to her exit from the stage, the lights went out, and I searched blindly for a tissue, knowing that tears were likely to fall again. Caleb reached over and took my hand to comfort me as Integer's video began painting big screens on either side of the room, and the message coming through the many speakers engulfed it.

I felt Caleb's hands begin to tremble in response to the deluge of tears falling from his eyes. He hadn't expected to be so overwhelmed upon hearing his surgeon's recorded words: "Caleb was a knife's edge between life and death." Flight for Life's turning blades then appeared on the screen and silently moved through the sky in slow motion as my mind flashed back to a farther distance two years ago…

The pilot's voice broke the room's silence, announcing their return to ground dispatch with words as eerily surreal: "Inbound Lifeguard One, skier collided with tree, requesting …" The audio fades, the screen goes black, and both stillness and pitch darkness fill the ballroom again. Large white letters slowly start to eat up the darkness as they appear on the screen and then come into focus for all to read: "The LORD is good, a refuge in times of trouble. He cares for those who trust in him" (Nahum 1:7). There were no dry eyes for any who had been involved in Caleb's recovery or the telling of HIStory. As I write today, my eyes again well up with tears at the wonder of it all.

We do not believe this is the end of this story, though it is the end of another semester. Caleb was provided an opportunity to share his story twice within the last month and to experience the way God continues to use him. Many times I've wondered where I would stop writing about the many events over the last two years, only to be provided with one more to share.

Caleb's two summer school sessions are now complete at College Station, and he will return home and take three online classes in the fall. If all goes as *planned*, he will graduate in December of 2014. We hold these plans loosely and pray to trust God's plans more than our own. We continue to know that our faith is in what is unseen, not what is seen, and He who began a good work in *all of us* will be faithful to carry it on to completion until the day when Jesus comes again.

Until then, life will come with many spills along the Way, so put on your helmet: the One who truly matters (Ephesians 6:17).

(Caleb graduated from Texas A&M on December 19, 2014, and worked for two years in ministry at iGo Global in Dallas, Texas.)

To God be the glory for the things He has done.

APPENDIX 1

RESOURCES

Jesus Calling by Sarah Young, a daily devotional

Jesus Today by Sarah Young, a daily devotional

Brain Storms: Recovery from Traumatic Brain Injury, by John W. Cassidy, MD

Mindstorms: The Complete Guide for Families Living with Traumatic Brain Injury by John W. Cassidy, MD

The Human Brain Book by Rita Carter

www.brainline.org – Glasgow Coma Scale; Rancho Los Amigos Scale

www.learningrx.com

www.lumosity.com

www.caringbridge.org/public/calebjentsch

St. Anthony Hospital, Lakewood, CO

TIRR Memorial Hermann, Houston, TX

Touchstone Neurorecovery Center, Conroe, TX

Warm Springs Rehabilitation, Victoria, TX

APPENDIX 2

SCRIPTURES: OUR SOURCE OF STRENGTH

The following scripture verses are quoted from the New International Version of the Bible.

"The LORD Is good, a refuge in times of trouble. He cares for those who trust in Him" (Nahum 1:7).

"May your unfailing love be with us, LORD, even as we put our hope in you" (Psalm 33:22).

"Look to the LORD and His strength; seek his face always" (Psalm 105:4).

"I will give you hidden treasures, riches stored in secret places, so that you may know that I am the LORD, the God of Israel who summons you by name" (Isaiah 45:3).

"I have told you these things, so that in me you may have peace. In this world you will have trouble. But take heart! I have overcome the world" (John 16:33).

"You turned my wailing into dancing; you removed my sackcloth and clothed me with joy, that my heart may sing your praises and not be silent. LORD my God, I will praise you forever" (Psalm 30:11–12).

"So do not fear, for I am with you; do not be dismayed, for I am your God. I will strengthen you and help you; I will uphold you with my righteous right hand" (Isaiah 41:10).

"Though the mountains be shaken and the hills be removed, yet my unfailing love for you will not be shaken nor my covenant of peace be removed, says the LORD, who has compassion on you" (Isaiah 54:10).

"On the evening of that first day of the week, when the disciples were together, with the doors locked for fear of the Jewish leaders, Jesus came and stood among them and said, 'Peace be with you!'" (John 20:19).

"Give thanks to the LORD, for he is good. *His love endures forever*" (Psalm 136:1).

"Trust in the LORD with all your heart and lean not on your own understanding;" (Proverbs 3:5).

"My comfort in my suffering is this: Your promise preserves my life" (Psalm 119:50).

"He will not let your foot slip—he who watches over Israel will neither slumber nor sleep" (Psalm 121:3–4).

"And my God will meet all your needs according to the riches of his glory Christ Jesus" (Philippians 4:19).

"For our light and momentary troubles are achieving for us an eternal glory that far outweighs them all" (2 Corinthians 4:17).

"He gives strength to the weary and increases the power of the weak" (Isaiah 40:29).

"Look to the LORD and his strength; seek his face always" (1 Chronicles 16:11).

"being confident of this, that he who began a good work in you will carry it on to completion until the day of Christ Jesus" (Philippians 1:6).

"If you, then, though you are evil, know how to give good gifts to your children, how much more will your Father in heaven give good gifts to those who ask him!" (Matthew 7:11).

"You shall have no other gods before me" (Exodus 20:3).

"...Rejoice with me; I have found my lost sheep" (Luke 15:6).

"You see, at just the right time, when we were still powerless, Christ died for the ungodly. Very rarely will anyone die for a righteous person, though for a good person someone might possibly dare to die. But God demonstrates his own love for us in this: While we were still sinners, Christ died for us" (Romans 5:6–8).

"Great is the LORD and most worthy of praise; his greatness no one can fathom. One generation commends your works to another; they tell of your mighty acts" (Psalm 145:3–4).

"Now the earth was formless and empty, darkness was over the surface of the deep, and the Spirit of God was hovering over the waters" (Genesis 1:2).

"Instead of your shame you will receive a double portion, and instead of disgrace you will rejoice in your inheritance. And so you will inherit a double portion in your land, and everlasting joy will be yours" (Isaiah 61:7).

"…You will see neither wind nor rain, yet this valley will be filled with water … And you will drink … And the land was filled with water" (2 Kings 3:17–20).

"LORD, I have heard of your fame; I stand in awe of your deeds, LORD. Repeat them in our day, in our time make them known; in wrath remember mercy" (Habakkuk 3:2).

"You have made known to me the paths of life; you will fill me with joy in your presence" (Acts 2:28).

"…You anoint my head with oil; my cup overflows" (Psalm 23:5).

"Now to him who is able to do immeasurably more than all we ask or imagine, according to his power that is at work within us, to him be glory in the church and in Christ Jesus throughout all generations, for ever and ever! Amen" (Ephesians 3:20–21).

"Therefore go and make disciples of all nations, baptizing them in the name of the Father and of the Son and of the Holy Spirit, and teaching them to obey everything I have commanded you. And surely I am with you always, to the very end of the age" (Matthew 28:19–20).

Take the helmet of salvation and the sword of the Spirit, which is the word of God. (Ephesians 6:17)

The following scripture verses are quoted from the English Standard Version of the Bible.

"Count it all joy, my brothers, when you meet trials of various kinds, for you know that the testing of your faith produces steadfastness. And let steadfastness have its full effect, that you may be perfect and complete, lacking in nothing" (James 1:2–4).

.."for all have sinned and fall short of the Glory of God" (Romans 3:23).

"For the wages of sin is death, but the free gift of God is eternal life in Christ Jesus our Lord" (Romans 6:23).

"And he said, My presence will go with you, and I will give you rest" (Exodus 33:14).

"Be still and know that I am God..." (Psalm 46:10).

"This is the day that the LORD has made; let us rejoice and be glad in it" (Psalm 118:24).

"...I will turn their mourning into joy; I will comfort them, and give them gladness for sorrow" (Jeremiah 31:13).

The following scripture verses are quoted from The Message.

"The fundamental fact of existence is that this trust in God, this faith, is the firm foundation under everything that makes life worth living. It's our handle on what we can't see" (Hebrews 11:1).

"By no means do I count myself an expert in all of this, but I've got my eye on the goal, where God is beckoning us onward—to Jesus. I'm off and running, and I'm not turning back" (Philippians 3:13).

"I am God. I have called you to live right and well. I have taken responsibility for you, kept you safe. I have set you among my people to bind them to me, and provided you as a lighthouse to the nations, To make a start at bringing people into the open, into light" (Isaiah 42:6–7).

"No test or temptation that comes your way is beyond the course of what others have had to face. All you need to remember is that God will never let you down; he'll never let you be pushed past your limit; he'll always be there to help you come through it" (1 Corinthians 10:13).

The following scripture verses are quoted from the New Living Translation of the Bible.

"Keep watch and pray, so that you will not give in to temptation. For the spirit is willing, but the body is weak!" (Matthew 26:41).

"...be strong and courageous! Do not be afraid or discouraged. For the LORD your God is with you wherever you go" (Joshua 1:9).

"Be still in the presence of the LORD, and wait patiently for him to act..." (Psalm 37:7).

"The LORD is merciful and compassionate, slow to get angry and filled with unfailing love" (Psalm 145:8).

"Our Father in heaven, may your name be kept holy.
May your Kingdom come soon.
May your will be done on earth, as it is in heaven.
Give us today the food we need, and forgive us our sins, as we have forgiven those who sin against us.
And don't let us yield to temptation, but rescue us from the evil one" (Matthew 6:9–13).
"For thine is the kingdom, and the power, and the glory for ever. Amen" (Matthew 6:13 KJV).

"How precious are your thoughts about me, O God. They cannot be numbered! I can't even count them; they outnumber the grains of sand! And when I wake up, you are still with me!" (Psalm 139:17–18).

"I will put my Spirit in you, and you will live again and return home to your own land. Then you will know that I, the LORD, have spoken, and I have done what I said. Yes, the LORD has spoken!" (Ezekiel 37:14).

"Don't let your hearts be troubled. Trust in God, and trust also in me. There is more than enough room in my Father's home. If this were not so, would I have told you that I am going to prepare a place for you? When everything is ready, I will come and get you, so that you will always be with me where I am" (John 14:1–3).

"...God will certainly come to help you ... Don't be afraid. Just stand still and watch the LORD rescue you ... and the LORD himself will fight for you..." (Exodus 13:19; 14:13–14).

The following scripture verses are quoted from the King James Version of the Bible.

"For even the Son of Man came not to be ministered unto, but to minister..." (Mark 10:45).

"But they that wait upon the LORD shall renew their strength;" (Isaiah 40:31).

"For thine is the kingdom, and the power, and the glory for ever. Amen" (Matthew 6:13).

The following scripture verses are quoted from additional translations of the Bible.

"You shall worship the Lord your God, and Him only shall you serve" (Matthew 4:10 NKJV).

"I will lift up my eyes to the mountains; From where shall my help come from? My help *comes* from the LORD, who made heaven and earth" (Psalm 121:1–2 NASB).

"Haven't I commanded you: be strong and courageous? Do not be afraid or discouraged, for the LORD your God is with you wherever you go" (Joshua 1:9 HCSB).

"...Buy from me medicine to put on your eyes so you can truly see" (Revelation 3:18 NCV).

"The LORD is good, giving protection in times of trouble. He knows who trusts in Him (Nahum 1:7 NCV).

"being confident of this very thing, that he who began a good work in you will perfect it until the day of Jesus Christ" (Philippians 1:6 ASV).

"Gracious is the LORD, and righteous; Yes, our God *is* merciful. The LORD preserves the simple; I was brought low, and He saved me. Return to your rest, O my soul, For the LORD has dealt bountifully with you" (Psalm 116:5–7 NKJV).

"Not to us, O LORD, not to us! But to your name bring honor, for the sake of your loyal love and faithfulness" (Psalm 115:1 NET).

Printed in the United States
By Bookmasters